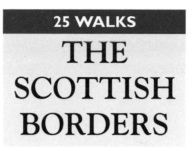

25 WALKS

THE SCOTTISH BORDERS

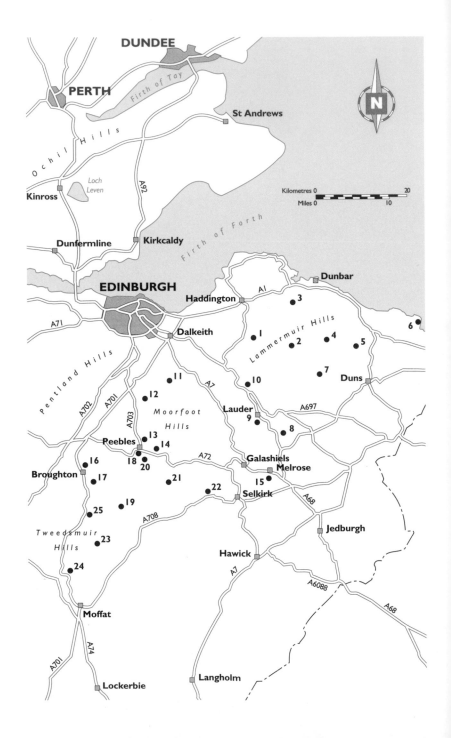

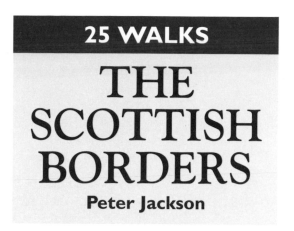

25 WALKS

THE SCOTTISH BORDERS

Peter Jackson

Series Editor: Roger Smith

Scottish Borders Enterprise

EDINBURGH:HMSO

Applications for reproduction should be made to HMSO

Acknowledgements

Thanks are due to the staff of Tourist Information Centres of the Scottish
Borders Tourist Board, The Borders Regional Council Ranger Service,
David Goss Associates and Forest Enterprise for help given during the
writing of this book.
HMSO acknowledges the financial assistance of Scottish Borders Enterprise
towards the publishing of this book. Thanks are also due to Scottish Borders
Tourist and Enterprise for vetting text and the supply of additional
transparencies (including the cover). Also to the author and editor for
supplying the bulk of the transparencies, and
Janet Widdicombe for the line illustration on page 103.

All facts have been checked as far as possible but the author and publishers
cannot be held respoinsible for any errors, however caused.

British Library Cataloguing in Publication Data

A catalogue record for this book is available from the British Library

Cover Illustration: The Eildon Hills

ISBN 0 11 495218 3

CONTENTS

USEFUL INFORMATION

The length of each walk is given in kilometres and miles, but within the text, measurements are metric for simplicity. The information panel contains details of each walk including the map number of the Ordnance Survey Landranger map at 1:50,000 which covers the walking area. These, together with the more detailed 1:25,000 Pathfinder series, are on sale locally and at Tourist Information Centres.

Every care has been taken to make the descriptions and maps as accurate as possible, but the author and publishers can accept no responsibility for errors, however caused. Many of the walks in this book are along Rights of Way, Drove Roads, sections of the Southern Upland Way (see below), and regularly used tracks. The description of a route in the text, and its representation on the accompanying map, does not however imply that it is a Right of Way.

Most of the walks in this book are not on 'official' or maintained paths, and neither the publisher nor the landowners can be held responsible for any injury or accident, however caused.

The countryside is always changing and there will inevitably be alterations to some aspect of these walks as times goes by. The publishers and author would be happy to receive comments and suggested alterations for future editions of the book.

Abbreviations
A number of abbreviations are used within the text. Usually these are explained, but a few, used frequently, are explained here.

OS: Ordnance Survey.
The OS is our national mapping agency, covering the whole of the UK at various scales. The two scales most frequently used by walkers are 1:25,000 and 1:50,000. All OS maps are drawn on a grid of kilometre squares.

SROWS: Scottish Rights of Way Society.
Established in 1845 and reconstituted in 1946, the objects of the society are (1) The preservation, defence and acquisition of public rights of way in Scotland; and (2) The erection and repair of bridges, guideposts, gates, stiles, etc. in connection with public rights of way. The author believes that

METRIC MEASUREMENTS

At the beginning of each walk, the distance is given in miles and kilometres. Within the text, all measurements are metric for simplicity (and indeed our Ordnance Survey maps are now all metric). However, it was felt that a conversion table might be useful to those readers who, like the author, still tend to think in Imperial terms.

The basic statistic to remember is that one kilometre is five-eighths of a mile. Half a mile is equivalent to 800 metres and a quarter-mile is 400 metres. Below that distance, yards and metres are little different in practical terms.

km	miles
1	0.625
1.6	1
2	1.25
3	1.875
3.2	2
4	2.5
4.8	3
5	3.125
6	3.75
6.4	4
7	4.375
8	5
9	5.625
10	6.25
16	10

all who walk in the Scottish countryside, should consider membership of the society, phone (0131) 652 2937 for details.

SUW: The Southern Upland Way
Scotland's 212 mile (340 km) cross-country route between Portpatrick in the west, and Cockburnspath on Berwickshire's North Sea coast. Approximately 90 miles (140 km) of this challenging long distance walk passes through Scotland's Border Region. The official guide to the SUW is now in its 2nd edition, written by Roger Smith, and published by HMSO.

General Information
For information on accommodation, travel and visitor attractions contact the Scottish Borders Tourist Board, Murray's Green, Jedburgh TD8 6BE. Tel: 01835 863688/863435, Fax: 01835 864099. Within the area covered by this book there are Tourist Information Centres in Peebles (01721 720138), Eyemouth (01890 750678), Galashiels (01896 755551) and Melrose (01896 822555). The Peebles TIC is open from Easter to end November, the others are open from Easter to end October. The TIC in Jedburgh (details above) is open all year.
East Lothian Tourist Board, Oldcraighall, Musselburgh (0131 653 6172) covers the area described in walks 1–4.

Walks Information
For further information on walking in the Scottish Borders, write to the Walking Development Officer, Scottish Borders Enterprise, Bridge Street, Galashiels TD1 1CW. A free walkers accommodation list is available on request.
The countryside rangers offer a comprehensive programme of guided walks throughout the year. Details and a free programme from Countryside Ranger Service, Harestanes Visitor Centre, Ancrum, Jedburgh (01835 830281).
For details of forest walks contact Forest Enterprise, Greenside, Peebles (01721 720448) or local forest offices. Leaflets are also available at Tourist Information Centres.

Public Transport
Free bus timetables can be obtained from Borders Regional Council, Regional Headquarters, Newtown St. Boswells TD6 0SA, or at Tourist Information Centres. In the summer the seasonal Harrier buses can be very useful to walkers. Enquire locally for details.

Equipment and Safety
Unlike other volumes in this series, this book mainly describes hill walks. Several rise to over 610 m (2000 ft) and are up to 20 km in length. Although the walks are fully described, it is essential that you have the proper equipment and clothing and are competent in the use of map and compass if tackling these hill walks. The maps which accompany the walks description are not sufficient in themselves in hill country, and an Ordnance Survey map should always be carried. Even in summer, the weather can change rapidly, and you should always take waterproof/windproof clothing and sufficient food and drink.

Although the Borders hills are in general much less craggy than those of the Highlands, they can still hold danger for the inexperienced, especially under snow or in mist, and in such conditions should only be tackled by suitably experienced walkers.

As elsewhere in Scotland, weather conditions in the Scottish Borders are variable. In general, the weather here is much drier than further west, and you are also less likely to be plagued by midges in summer. The driest times of year are usually May, June, September and October, and a visit in spring or autumn can be especially rewarding, with the colouring at its best.

Dogs

Many people enjoy the company of a dog on their walks. Unfortunately, dogs are a major cause of concern for farmers and landowners, especially at sensitive times of the year such as the lambing season (March to May).

If you wish to bring your dog, please keep it under very close control. In livestock areas dogs must be kept on a lead at all times. At the most sensitive times such as lambing, it is better to leave your dog at home. We can do no better than to quote the well-known writer Hamish Brown (a contributor to this series): "There is hardly a day when a dog would not present problems or be most unwelcome to farmers and shepherds. I say this as a fanatic dog-owner but feel affection enough for my dog *not* to take him along. Try a two-legged friend instead!"

Dogs are not permitted on some of the walks described in this book, and where this applies, a note has been added to the text. Please note also that dogs are not allowed on the ranger-led walks.

Shooting

Grouse shooting, an important source of income and employment for estates and farms, takes place over many of the hills covered in this book. The management of the moorland for grouse helps to ensure that the heather, one of the principal attractions for the walker, remains healthy.

The grouse shooting season starts on 12 August (often called the Glorious Twelfth) and runs through to late October. Shooting does not take place every day, but during this period it is advisable to seek local advice before going onto the hills. A courteous enquiry will usually lead to advice as to where you can walk without disturbing the shooting activity.

During the early spring, areas of heather are burnt to encourage fresh growth and thus provide food for the young birds. This burning does not normally interfere with access, but if you do come across heather burning while following any of the routes in the book, please ask if a diversion is necessary.

The Country Code

Please follow the Country Code while out walking. In particular:

- Leave gates as you find them, and be especially careful to close any gate you have to open;
- Never drop litter, and if possible pick up litter which others have carelessly discarded;
- Respect the life and work of the countryside.

INTRODUCTION

This book describes 25 mainly circular walks in the Lammermuir, Moorfoot and Tweedsmuir Hills. The Eildon Hills which lie just outside these ranges are also included. Each of these upland areas have distinctive characteristics which makes walking in them a particular pleasure.

The Lammermuir Hills, which have their eastern feet in the North Sea, are separated from the Moorfoot Hills by the A7 road. Although rising to a maximum height of only 533 m these heather clad hills contain many a hidden stretch of water, secret hill burns and a wealth of historic and pre-historic sites. This is grouse country and walkers should take care not to disturb nesting birds, and during the shooting season, starting on the 12 August, be prepared to wait until drives are over before proceeding.

The Moorfoot Hills are separated from the Tweedsmuir Hills by the River Tweed. These are higher hills than the Lammermuirs, particularly in the west, where they provide excellent views towards the Pentland Hills south of Edinburgh. Glentress Forest is a particular feature of the southern Moorfoots. Covering an area of 1140 hectares, Glentress is the oldest of Forest Enterprise forests in the south of Scotland, with the earliest plantings dating from 1920.

The Tweedsmuir Hills, which include the Manor Hills south of Peebles, lie south of the River Tweed and east of the A701. Here are some of the highest hills in the south of Scotland, providing outstanding views in all directions. It is a land of deep valleys and shining waters. Along the way you walk in the footsteps of poets, wizards, kings and fighting men.

You may walk all day in the Border hills and not meet a soul along the way. Even in these remote areas however, there are those who earn their living among the lonely hills and glens. Shepherds, gamekeepers, farmers, foresters and drystane dykers, may all be met on your various walks. Most will welcome a friendly chat and be interested in where you have come from, and where you are walking to.

Sheep predominate throughout Scotland's Border Region. There are some 1.4 million of them, and only 102,000 of us! Sheep and dogs don't mix, and walkers must be prepared to keep their dogs under close control, particularly at lambing time. Better by far to leave them at home during this period. Many of the walks in the Border hills will be through mature and newly planted forests, both publicly and privately owned. Do nothing to endanger such valuable assets. LIGHT NO FIRES under any circumstance and do not smoke at all in forest areas.

The 25 walks within this book are my own personal selection. They are intended to provide the walker with but a sample of the hill walking possibilities in Scotland's beautiful and romantic Border hills. Although not a "Borderer" myself, I have walked these hills for many years, and I hope that through this book, you will come to share my love for this very special and unique corner of Scotland.

PETER JACKSON

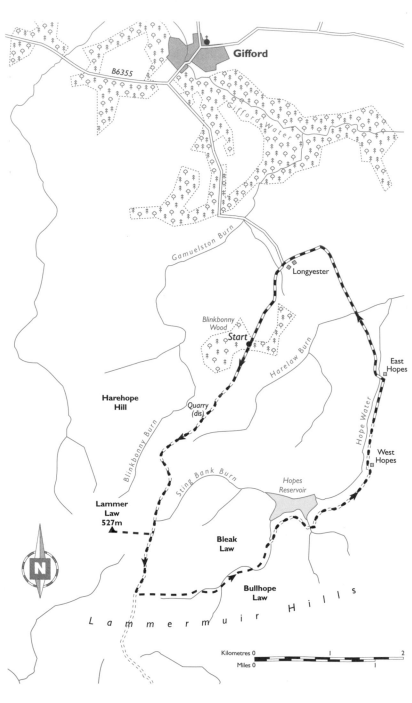

Gifford

B6355

Gifford Water

Gamuelston Burn

Longyester

Blinkbonny Wood

Start

Harelaw Burn

East Hopes

Harehope Hill

Quarry (dis)

Blinkbonny Burn

Hope Water

West Hopes

Sting Bank Burn

Hopes Reservoir

Lammer Law 527m

Bleak Law

Bullhope Law

L a m m e r m u i r   H i l l s

N

Kilometres 0   1   2

Miles 0   1

GIFFORD AND THE HOPES RESERVOIR

G ifford would be a leading contender in any competition for East Lothian's most attractive village. Gateway to the northern Lammermuir Hills, it has one of the prettiest churches in the south of Scotland. Gifford is an interesting example of a "planned" village. Towards the end of the 17th century, the Marquis of Tweeddale was laying out extensive plantations and parks in preparation for the rebuilding of his mansion. The settlement of Bothans, complete with its church, was inconveniently close to the "big house", so the Marquis had it moved to a site outside the gates of his new park. In 1708 he had a parish church built for the transferred village, on the site which still dominates the short main street of Gifford. The church bell in Yester Kirk, which is rung every Sunday, dates from 1492 and survives from the earlier building at Bothans.

To reach the start of the walk, drive down Gifford's main street and head west along the B6355. Just outside the village turn left, and follow the signs for Longyester. As you approach the farm of Longyester, take the second road on the right signposted to "Lammerlaw 2¾ miles, Carfraemill 8½ miles, Lauder 12¼ miles Impassable for motors". East Lothian District and Lothian Regional Councils are to be commended for maintaining these old cast iron "finger post" road signs in the rural areas. Some of the signs

INFORMATION

Distance: 11 km (7 miles).

Map: OS Landranger, sheet 66.

Start and finish: In Blinkbonny Wood at GR541642.

Terrain: Mainly on hill tracks and country lanes. One short section without path (no stiles, but a few gates and some streams to cross). Boots or strong shoes advised.

Refreshments: None en route. Two hotels in Gifford

Public transport: Bus service Edinburgh/ Gifford.

The Church at Gifford.

still have their round tops proclaiming "East Lothian *County* Council". Note the accuracy of this particular sign which states, Edinburgh 20⅝ miles! In 1 km along this lane, and on the right, there is a suitable parking space at the entrance to Blinkbonny Wood.

Continue walking up the road to a metal gate which leads out onto the open moor. Follow the broad rubble track firstly uphill, then turning neither right nor left, down across a flat rather marshy area, and uphill onto the north-east shoulder of Lammer Law. As the now grassy track makes a big left-hand bend, look back over the plain of East Lothian.

Given a clear day it will be possible to pick out such landmarks as North Berwick Law, the Bass Rock off North Berwick, away north-west towards Edinburgh, and beyond. What will certainly be seen, 13 km to the north, is the distinctive whale-backed shape of Traprain Law. This hill, which dominates the East Lothian plain, has signs of occupation probably from as early as 1500BC. What is more certain is that when the Romans arrived here around AD80, the fortifications on Traprain were the stronghold of the Votadini, a tribe whose sphere of influence stretched from the Firth of Forth to the River Tyne.

Higher up, the path is joined by a wire fence coming up the ridge above the Hopes Reservoir, which may now be glimpsed between the hills. Follow the track, with the fence to your left, to arrive at a large new gate

Road sign at Long Yester.

complete with an equally large new sign stating "PUBLIC RIGHT OF WAY LAUDER TO HADDINGTON. IN THE INTERESTS OF CONSERVATION PLEASE KEEP TO THE PATH AND KEEP DOGS ON A LEAD. F.E.L." (Faecombe Estates Ltd.). Beyond the gate and with the fence now on the right, the path levels out and passes to the east of Lammer Law. Through a gate in the fence an excursion may be made to the summit of Lammer Law (527 m). It has a flat top, and apart from the views to the north and west, it is not a particularly interesting summit. The trig point and summit cairn are 500 m from the gate.

The main track continues, now downhill, to arrive at a second large gate with a stile over the fence nearby. Do not go through the gate but follow the fence, still on your right, for some 200 m. At this point (GR526609) bear off to the left, away from the fence, through the heather, and descend a steep gully by the left hand side of an infant hill burn. Go down the steep sided gully with care to arrive in a flat grassy area between the hills. Walk forward across this flat area keeping generally to the left. Soon a clear track will materialise which, after passing to the right of some old sheep pens, heads for a green painted corrugated iron sheepfold and a nearby shed. Cross a stream, turn left past the green shed, and follow the improving track through the hills. Soon pass another large corrugated iron sheepfold and continue downhill to cross the much larger stream which now has a name – Hopes Water. Beyond the stream follow the track above the southern shore of the secluded Hopes Reservoir, built in the 1930s to supply the towns and villages of East Lothian.

The reservoir and its surroundings is an attractive place. Grouse abound on the hills and moors, hares are numerous, and many hives of bees are brought up to the heather in the

Fishing boats at the Hopes.

autumn. The reservoir is stocked with brown trout and a permit to fish, with use of boat, is available only from the Water Board office in Haddington. Beyond the dam end follow a broad track downhill for 1.5 km to reach the surfaced road beyond the water department buildings. Continue along the road as it turns left over a bridge and then right up through trees and open farmland. In 2 km turn left at the T-junction for Longyester. Pass through the farm and turn left again for Blinkbonny Wood.

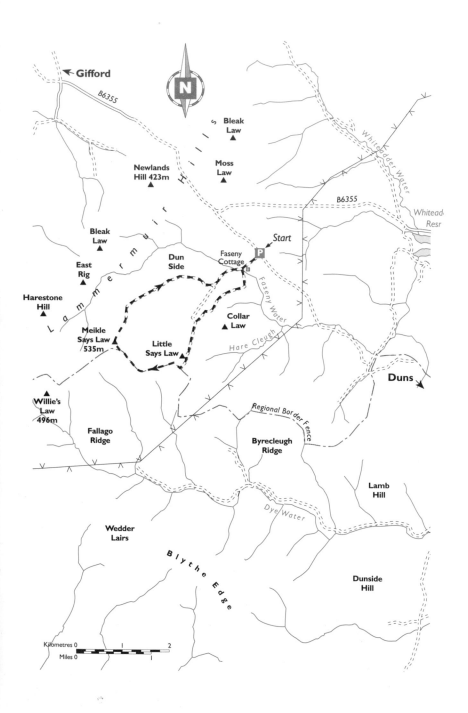

Gifford

B6355

N

Bleak
Law

Moss
Law

Newlands
Hill 423m

Whiteadder Water

B6355

Whitead
Resr

Bleak
Law

Dun
Side

Faseny
Cottage

Start

P

East
Rig

L a m m e r m u i r

Faseny Water

Harestone
Hill

Collar
Law

Meikle
Says Law
535m

Little
Says Law

Hare Cleugh

Duns

Willie's
Law
496m

Fallago
Ridge

Regional Border Fence

Byrecleugh
Ridge

Lamb
Hill

Dye Water

Wedder
Lairs

B l y t h e   E d g e

Dunside
Hill

Kilometres 0   1   2
Miles 0   1

MEIKLE SAYS LAW

This is an outing to the highest point in the Lammermuir Hills, following mainly good vehicle tracks and along a stretch of the regional boundary fence. In this part of the Lammermuirs, the heather-clad hills are a patchwork of colour. This is grouse country and the heather is burned rotationally to produce deep heather for nesting, and young heather shoots for the birds to feed on.

If you come this way in late winter or early spring you may see patches or strips of old heather ablaze and plumes of smoke seen from afar. The shooting of grouse and the management of their environment is an important source of employment and income in the area. Shooting starts on 12th August and from then until mid October, permission should be sought for this walk.

The walk starts at GR613637 on the unclassified road between the B6355 south-east of Gifford and the village of Longformacus. There is room for a car or two on the grass opposite the access gate. The gate will in all probability be padlocked but the wooden fence on the right is easily climbed. A steep but broad track descends to Faseny Cottage which sits above the Faseny Water. The stream, which flows directly into the Whiteadder Reservoir, is typical of many of

INFORMATION

Distance: 10 km (6 miles).

Map: OS Landranger, sheet 67.

Start and finish: At GR613637 on the unclassified road between Longformacus and the B6355. Parking opposite access gate.

Terrain: Mainly on good vehicle tracks. Some pathless walking in heather. Some streams to cross. Boots or strong shoes advised.

Refreshments: None en route. Good facilities in Duns and Gifford.

Public transport: None.

Muirburn near Faseny Cottage.

Lammermuir's secret waters. Most of the main streams and their tributaries cut quite deeply into these moorland hills and their discovery is always a delight.

The track divides near Faseny Cottage, both branches fording the stream 100 m or so apart. Take the left fork, cross the footbridge below the cottage and head

Faseny Water at footbridge.

uphill on a good track. After a sharp right-hand bend the route goes over the northern shoulder of Collar Law and down to cross a small hill burn. Continue uphill again and keeping straight ahead at a junction, follow the fading track to the 478 m top of Little Says Law.

Cross over the hill to reach the regional border fence. The fence, which has Lothian Region to its north, and Borders Region to its south, can be a good navigation

Track over Collar Law heading for Little Says Law.

aid in the Lammermuirs. Turn right and follow the fence for 1.5 km to the 535 m summit of Meikle Says Law. To call it a summit is rather a misnomer, the highest point in the Lammermuir Hills being to say the least, something of a disappointment.

On a clear day however, there are extensive views over the surrounding moorland. If you have both OS Landranger sheets 66 and 67, together with compass in hand, you will be able to identify a number of landmarks. Some 13 km to the south east are the twin peaks of Dirrington Great Law and Dirrington Little Law. Just west of south can be seen the Eildon Hills beyond Melrose.

Willie's Law is a short 1.5 km to the southwest. Willie must have been an important chap, since the region/county fence goes round the hill in order to keep him in Berwickshire! To the north-west lies the steep edge of the Lammermuir Hills. This feature, together with the similar north-western edge of the Moorfoot Hills, clearly locates the line of the Dunbar/Girvan geological fault. Along Lammermuir Edge are a number of prehistoric forts and cairns. Newlands Hill is prominent to the north.

The return path from Meikle Says is at first indistinct. Head north-east from the trig point over gently sloping ground to pick up a track going downhill on the broad ridge over Dun Side. The track now swings east above the Lamb Burn. After passing through a line of grouse butts it joins a much broader vehicle track. Keep left at a junction and walk downhill to ford the Faseny Water, or cross the smaller Lamb Burn to reach the footbridge below Faseny Cottage. Head uphill to your waiting car.

If time allows, a longer expedition may be made by heading north-west from Meikle Says Law for 1.5 km to the Whitestone Cairn on Harestone Hill (GR568623). Turn north-east along the Lammermuir edge, over East Rig, Bleak Law and over Newlands Hill to reach the B6355 road. The views to the north-west over the plain of East Lothian, to the Pentland Hills and to the Firth of Forth and beyond, are particularly fine. On reaching the road turn right, and keeping right at a junction, walk the 3 km back to your car.

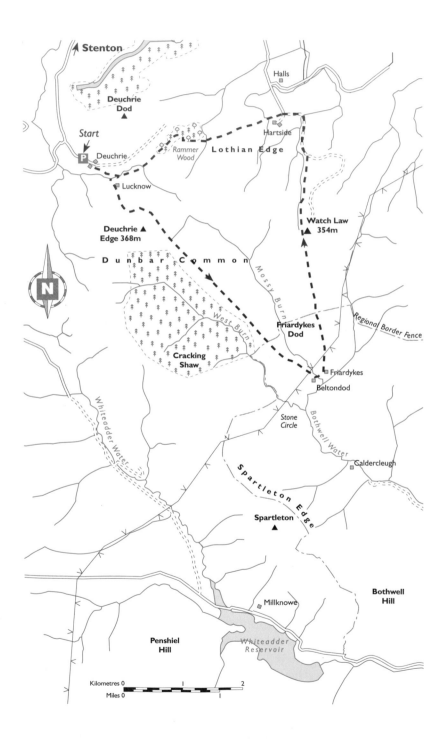

DUNBAR COMMON

There are a number of useful Rights of Way through the Lammermuir Hills and this walk makes use of two of the longer ones. Initially it follows part of the route from East Linton to Cranshaws, and later a section of the 47 km Herring Road between Dunbar and Lauder.

The farm house of Deuchrie is a fine building and lies on the edge of the Lammermuir Hills 3 km south of Stenton, an agricultural village on the B6370 midway between Dunbar and Gifford. A car may be parked on the broad left verge in front of empty farm cottages. Walk through the yard in front of the house, go through a gate, and head downhill on a wide farm track. After crossing a small burn continue uphill, passing to the right of the abandoned house of Lucknow. Did the builder or an occupant see service during the Indian Mutiny of 1857?

The track now climbs more steeply up towards Deuchrie Edge. Near an old stone sheepfold the track swings left and continues upwards before levelling out onto the open moor of Dunbar Common. Look back

INFORMATION

Distance: 14 km (8.5 miles).

Map: OS Landranger, sheet 67.

Start and Finish: Deuchrie Farm (GR623714). From the west end of Stenton on B6370, turn south on a minor road past Pressmennan Wood. In 2.5 km, at a sharp right-hand bend, turn left for Deuchrie.

Terrain: Hill and farm tracks. Boots recommended, particularly in wet weather.

Refreshments: None en route. Ample facilities in Dunbar.

Public transport: None.

The Hopetoun Monument, a well-known East Lothian landmark.

here for extensive views over the plain of East Lothian and beyond. Easily spotted landmarks include the conical shape of North Berwick Law and the whaleback outline of Traprain. Further left, the Hopetoun Monument on the Garleton Hills above Haddington is a prominent East Lothian landmark seen from viewpoints both near and far. Arthur's Seat in Edinburgh and the Pentland Hills to the south of the city are also clearly in view.

Up to now the track has been clear and easy to follow. As it heads out onto the moor, however, it becomes more indistinct. Although a Right of Way and clearly marked on the map, the path is not so easily followed on the ground. In the first instance follow a path which developed on the left, parallel to the disappearing main track. There is the odd large stone beside the path which would seem to indicate the line of the old way. Keep heading south-east and beyond a ditch, and a marshy bit of ground, make for a conspicuous iron fence post set into a large stone and near to the corner of a wire fence.

Beyond the old iron post walk forward to the left of the wire fence. Some twelve metres or so to the left of the fence a track develops in the heather, gradually improving as it heads for an iron gate in a cross fence. Climb over the gate and walk forward to the left of the continuing wire fence.

Near to fence junctions can be seen old marker stones which before fences, marked the limits of land ownership. At least one such stone has an Ordnance Survey bench mark on its surface. Come eventually to a complicated set of gates. Walk down the now very obvious track beyond, still keeping to your left the wire fence which now bounds the recently planted forest of Cracking Shaw.

It is difficult to imagine that moorland like Dunbar Common was once under cultivation and crops of cereals grown. In medieval time when much of the lower land was heavily forested it was easier to clear the more thinly covered high ground. The climate was also much drier than at any time since. The falling population following the Black Death may well have started the decline and abandonment of these holdings. From the 14th century onwards the climate became colder and wetter, driving the limits of cultivation downhill. By the mid 18th century, the high land was forsaken and much uncultivated land at lower levels was brought under the plough.

At the end of the fence the track swings right. Leave the track and continue ahead through tussocky grass to reach a gate in a cross fence. Climb over the gate and walk down a broad ride between young trees to reach a bulldozed track. Bear left and after passing through a double gate walk down under power lines to reach the old abandoned farmstead of Beltondod. Turn left here and after crossing the Mossy Burn walk up towards the cottage and buildings of Friardykes.

Beltondod, deep in the Lammermuirs.

Just before Friardykes, cut up left through a gate and walk up the obvious track behind the cottage. The building has been restored over the years and is now lived in at weekends. In some 200 m and almost directly under power lines go through a gate on the left and walk up a path to the left of a long strip of trees. At the north end of the narrow plantation cross a stile to the left of a gate, and keeping to the right of a wire fence head uphill towards the 354 m summit of Watch Law.

Just over the top of the hill pass to the right of sheep pens, through a gate, and start downhill on a distinct track through grass and heather. Where the main track swings right, take a left fork and follow a well defined path down to the right of a developing hill burn.

Lammermuir hill burn.

Lower down go through a gate and rejoin the main track which has come down from the right. Bear left here and walk down through a couple of gates to meet a stone wall. Turn left through a gate and walk beside the wall, cross the road leading to the cottages of Hartside, and head for the wooden gate beyond.

Through the gate a track leads down to some wooden sheep pens. Pass through the three gates in the pens, turn left through a metal gate and turn sharp right. An obvious path leads through a small valley with extensive scree slopes on a little hill to the right of the path. Follow the clear track as it skirts round a dried out pond, beyond which, it heads up left to meet a wire fence. Walk up beside the fence for 1 km (10/15 mins) to a point where it meets a wall on the right and where there is a large cairn-like pile of stones on the left.

Ahead, and beyond a small hill burn, there is a metal gate half hidden in gorse bushes. Cross the burn, pass through the gate, and walk up the somewhat overgrown track beyond. As soon as open grassland is reached, turn half right and head down towards the southern edge of Rammer Wood.

Before long a tractor track will be met. Turn left and follow the track as it skirts round a rather boggy area before heading for a well defined track leading down into Rammer Wood. Walk down the track, passing to the right of an iron shed, to reach the valley floor. Cross over to a wire fence, turn left, and follow the track to the end of the wood. Leave the wooded area by a gate and follow a track across a couple of fields to reach the main track below Lucknow. Turn right and walk up to Deuchrie and your waiting car.

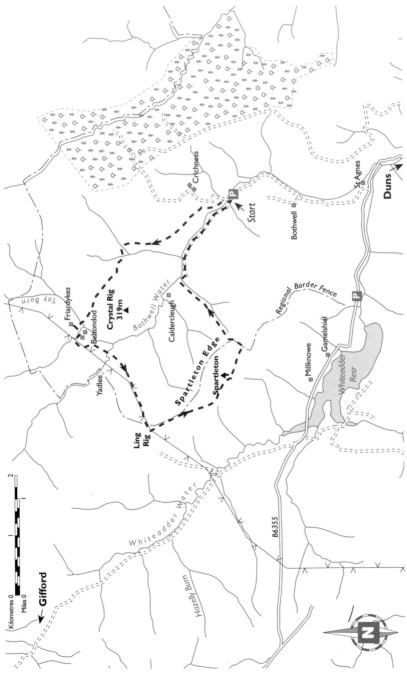

Crichness

St Agnes

Duns

P

Start

Bothwell

Regional Border Fence

P

Tay Burn

Friardykes

Beltondod

Crystal Rig 319m

Bothwell Water

Caldercleugh

Gamelshiel

Millknowe

Whiteadder Resr

Yadlee

Spartleton Edge

Spartleton

Ling Rig

Whiteadder Water

B6355

Hazelly Burn

Gifford

Kilometres 0

Miles 0

2

N

BOTHWELL WATER AND SPARTLETON EDGE

This most interesting walk is almost completely within the bounds of Berwickshire. It does however stray briefly into East Lothian, and the summit of Spartleton is within that District. It encircles the headwaters of the Bothwell Water, a tributary of the Whiteadder Water, and visits abandoned farmsteads on the edge of Dunbar Common.

The start is reached off the B6355 Gifford to Duns road. Some 2 km east of the dam end of the Whiteadder reservoir follow the sign for Bothwell, Crichness and Elmscleugh. Drive uphill, pass the farm of Bothwell, and follow the road along the left bank of the busy Bothwell Water. Park at any convenient spot on the wide grassy area on either side of the road, just before it crosses a bridge over the river. Take care not to obstruct any gateway on the left.

Walk over the concrete bridge and almost immediately turn left through a metal gate, beside a corrugated iron shed. Follow the broad track fairly steeply uphill to reach another metal gate with a stile at its right hand side. There is a sign beyond the gate which reads "FOLLOW GREEN MARKERS. PUBLIC FOOTPATH TO CRAIGBURN PICNIC SITE ¼ MILE. APPROPRIATE FOOTWEAR PLEASE".

Continue uphill along the edge of the recently planted forest. Note from here the track below, on the far side of the Bothwell Water. This track will be used on the return journey from Spartleton. Your track swings away right and meets a sign proclaiming "PICNIC SITE". The sign points left in the direction of a ride through newly planted woodland. The very faint path is obviously not well trodden and the picnic site must be little used.

Stride out, now along the well made forestry track. At a T-junction, near to an old railway wagon (where do

INFORMATION

Distance: 10.5 km (6.5 miles).

Map: OS Landranger, sheet 67.

Start and finish: On grass beside the Bothwell Water at approx. GR682654.

Terrain: Good tracks and hill paths. Boots or strong footwear advised.

Refreshments: None en route. Ample facilities in Gifford, Duns or Dunbar.

Public transport: None.

Note: The recently planted Crystal Forest is walked through by consent of the landowner. Light no fires and no smoking please.

they all come from?), turn left on to the line of the original track which comes down the hill from Crichness Law. Further along the track, at another T-junction below a small reservoir, turn left again. This is a new reservoir, presumably built to provide a supply of water for forest fire fighting purposes. All around the area of Crystal Rig are extensive new forest plantings.

The track heads uphill keeping to the left of a small, mature plantation. Over a rise the landscape is somewhat marred by the sight of pylons and power lines marching over the moor from the direction of Torness nuclear power station, south-east of Dunbar. The cottage of Friardykes, and the old farm buildings of Beltondod, soon came into view.

Close to the cottage, cross the Tay Burn by a bridge of sleepers, and pass through a blue metal gate. Follow the path left at Friardykes, cross a stream and walk up towards Beltondod. The old farm buildings are now used as a feed store and for sheep rearing activities. At Beltondod the track turns sharp right and goes over a cattle grid almost directly beneath the power lines. Beyond the cattle grid the track turns left and continues parallel to the power lines.

Spartleton Hill from the west.

Further on the track swings left, then right, to cross the West Burn near to a caravan, used as a bothy by local shepherds. Beyond the stream the track generally follows the line of pylons up towards the ridge and Ling Rig. The "road" that has been followed from Beltondod was constructed for the installation of pylons and transmission lines, and is still used as an access road to service and maintain them.

Near the ridge pass through two sets of gates, a hundred metres or so apart. At the second pylon beyond the second gate, turn hard left on to a clear grass path, and head along Spartleton Edge towards Spartleton Hill. As you walk up the ridge, note that the boundary fence goes round the north-east shoulder of the hill, and that the most prominent path heads away south. The path to aim for goes up the centre of the hill ahead.

Walk uphill and follow the path as it swings right and then left, south of the summit. Just as the path starts downhill, turn sharp left for the trig point and the prehistoric summit burial cairn. From this vantage point North Berwick Law, and the Bass Rock, can be clearly seen away to the north-east. Walk back to the main track for good views of the Whiteadder Reservoir, built in the 1960s to satisfy an increasing water demand from the towns and villages of East Lothian.

Bass Rock, North Berwick

Walk downhill to a gate in our old friend, the border fence. Don't pass through the gate, but turn left, and follow an obvious path beside the fence. In 200/300 m,

The Whiteadder Reservoir.

arrive at a junction of fences. Cross over the fence ahead, to the left of a rusty old gate. Walk away from the fence, and in 25/30 m meet a distinct cross path. Turn left, and in a further 25/30 m turn right and follow a track down the ridge to the left of a steep sided gully.

Walk on down the ridge on a clear track, keeping always to the left of the gully, to arrive at a fence above the Bothwell Water. Turn down right here and follow the track along the right hand bank of the river, firstly through a little gorge and then across a pleasant grass field. Pass through a gate to the right of the bridge over which you walked some three hours or more ago.

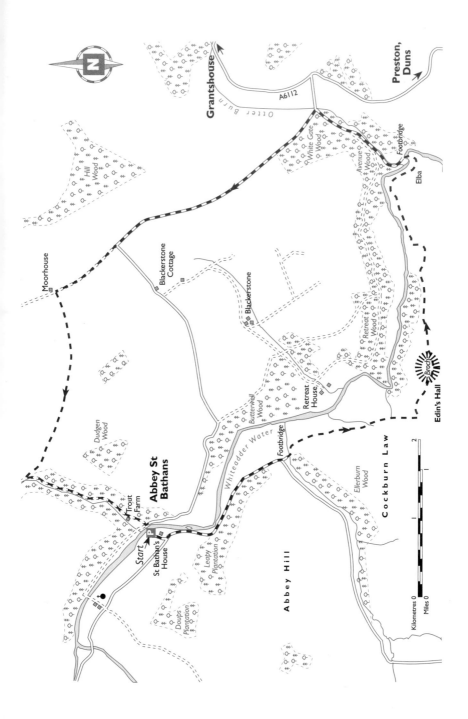

ABBEY ST BATHANS AND EDIN'S HALL BROCH

The estate village of Abbey St Bathans nestles in the valley of the Whiteadder Water, some 12 km north of Duns and a similar distance south of Cockburnspath. The name of the village is shrouded in mystery. Tradition has it that a chapel was erected here in the 7th century by a visiting missionary by the name of Bothan or St Bathan. What is more certain is that towards the end of the 12th century, a priory of 12 cistercian nuns was founded here by Ada, a daughter of William the Lion. The priory was virtually destroyed by an English army in 1543, the east gable and north wall being incorporated in the present Parish Church. It seems certain that neither the chapel nor the priory ever attained "abbey" status and its use as part of the village name remains something of a mystery. The valley here is said to contain almost a third of all oak woods in the Border Region and there are rhododendrons in profusion.

To start the walk, turn left out of the trout farm car park and head south-east along the unclassified road out of the village. In just over 1 km, where the road takes a sharp right hand bend is a road sign never seen in the Highway Code. It simply says "TOOT"! Go through a small gate on the left and follow a short stepped path down to a bridge over a stream. Cross

INFORMATION

Distance: 9.7 km (6 miles).

Time: 3 hours.

Map: OS Landranger, sheet 67.

Start and finish: Parking available near trout farm and tearoom. Limited parking in lane by the church.

Terrain: Country lanes, forest and field tracks (there are a couple of awkward wooden steps over walls. Strong footwear advised.

Refreshments: None en route. "The Riverside" in Abbey St Bathans sells morning coffee, lunches and cream teas.

Public transport: Early morning Post Bus from Duns (01361) 882292. School bus to and from Duns (01835) 823301 ext 523 for details.

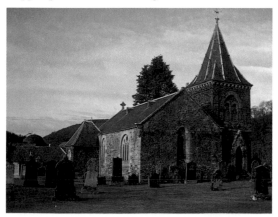

Abbey St Bathans Kirk.

over the stile beyond the bridge and follow the clear path going left. Soon the path bends right uphill, away from the stream and heads south-east over open ground. Keep always to the main path, firstly along a fairly level section, then rising steadily to reach a wooden gate leading into a field. Beyond the gate turn left, and walk downhill to reach a gate set in a wire fence. Once through the gate go right, and head uphill on a somewhat indistinct path to reach the impressive Edin's Hall Broch on the rise.

Edin's Hall Broch.

The broch is one of only ten such fortified buildings in the south of Scotland. It dates from the 2nd century AD and is situated within the earthen ramparts and ditches of a much earlier settlement. The Iron Age Broch measures 25 m in diameter with its walls varying in thickness between 4 m and 6 m. Within the walls are a series of cells and chambers, which can provide shelter for your lunch on a windy day. The walls now stand at an average height of only 1.5 m, most of the building having been dismantled in the past to build drystone dykes. Look on the far bank of the Whiteadder for the circular building known as Retreat House. This was built in the late 18th century by the Earl of Wemyss as a hunting or shooting lodge.

To continue the walk, head due east from the broch and follow a clear path downhill to a grey metal swing gate. You'll almost certainly have to remove your rucksack to squeeze through! The path continues, with a wire fence and trees on your left to arrive at a wall with wooden steps set into it. Take care, as in wet conditions the steps can be fairly slippery. On this section of the walk you will see signs pointing to Edin's

Hall Broch in the direction from which you have just come. Don't be confused – another popular route to the broch is from a parking spot in Elba Wood. After crossing the wall, follow the path along a ridge above the river and, passing beneath power lines, arrive at a second wall also with wooden steps and equally slippery. Over the wall turn left, then right, to follow a wire fence along the south bank of the Whiteadder. At a junction, keep to the lower left-hand track and pass through a gate. The path now swings left behind the cottages of Elba and crosses the river by an attractive footbridge.

Once over the bridge turn left. After crossing a small feeder stream the track swings right and heads uphill to arrive at a junction with a country lane. Turn left here, and walk uphill for 2 km to reach a road junction at Moorhouse. Go left opposite the house, climb over a stile, and follow a clear track down the side of Edgar's Cleugh to reach the Whare Burn. The track now meets the Southern Upland Way as it leaves the shelter of the Whiteadder valley, and heads for its final destination (or its start!) at Cockburnspath, on Berwickshire's North Sea coast. Turn left and walk beside the burn by track and country lane down to the Whiteadder and Abbey St Bathans. Cross the river by the ford or the footbridge, both leading into the car parking area near the trout farm – and the Riverside Restaurant.

The Southern Upland Way crosses the Whiteadder Water by a footbridge built by Gurkhas in 1987. This replaced a previous elegant little suspension bridge which had fallen into disrepair. The 'Way' makes a number of interesting walks possible from the village including a route over Abbey Hill to the B6355 returning via SUW along the banks of the Whiteadder Water.

Bridge over the Whiteadder.

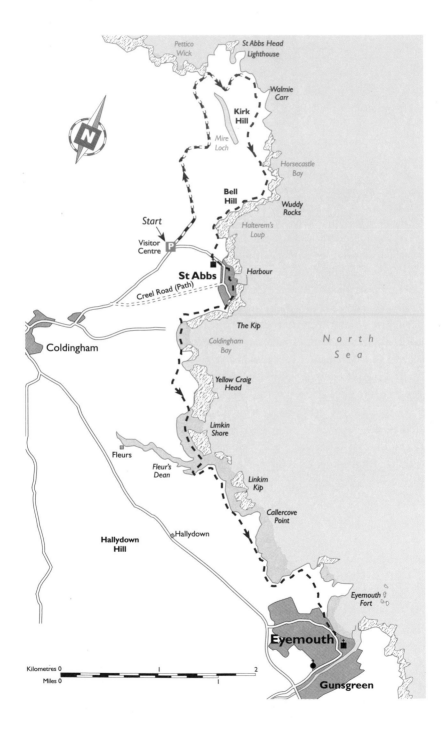

ST ABBS TO EYEMOUTH

The Berwickshire coast features a range of dramatic cliffs, reaching to over 150 m in several places. The birdlife is extensive and varied, and the coastal settlements interesting. This walk is therefore very satisfying on several counts.

It starts from the small Visitor Centre for the St Abbs Head National Nature Reserve. The reserve extends to 192 acres and is managed jointly by the National

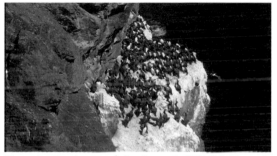

Trust for Scotland and the Scottish Wildlife Trust. It is one of the most important breeding areas for cliff-nesting seabirds in Scotland and at most times of the year the air is full of the sound of thousands of pairs of guillemots, kittiwakes, razorbills, shags, fulmars and herring gulls. You may also see puffin here. The offshore waters, which are popular with divers (of the human as well as avian kind) are a voluntary marine reserve.

The Visitor Centre, which has interesting displays on the wildlife and geology of the area, is open throughout the summer months. Next to it is the Head Start coffee shop, which, denying its name, may well delay your departure.

When you do start, turn right out of the carpark through Northfield Farm and continue along the single-track road to Pettico Wick. Partway along, down to the right you can see the Mire Loch, which has its own, different range of birds. The grassland here is managed for wildlife, and in summer you will see many butterflies.

INFORMATION

Distance: 9 km (5.5 miles).

Map: OS Landranger, sheet 67.

Start: St Abbs Head Visitor Centre, on B6438 500 m west of St Abbs village.

Finish: Eyemouth.

Terrain: Good paths and tracks. Strong footwear advised, as the path is near the cliff edge in several places.

Refreshments: Cafe at start. Good range of facilities in both St Abbs and Eyemouth.

Public transport: Frequent bus service between Eyemouth and St Abbs.

Opening hours: St Abbs Head Visitor Centre: Open daily, Easter to end Sept. Eyemouth Museum: Easter to end Sept., Mon-Sat 1000–1700, Sun 1400–1700.

Top: Seabirds nesting at St Abbs Head.

Below: St Abbs Head.

St Abbs Head Lighthouse.

In about 2 km you reach the cliffs at Pettico Wick, a point much used by divers. The northward view along the cliffs is dramatic. You are actually standing on the St Abbs Fault, with Devonian lavas to your right on the headland and Silurian muds and silts to your left. These rocks formed on the seabed over 400 million years ago.

Follow the road up to the lighthouse which, like most of its kind, is now automatic in operation. Turn south and follow the clear cliff path; the scenery is glorious and you will be accompanied by wheeling, diving, crying birds.

The path goes over a couple of smaller headlands and around Horsecastle Bay, Wuddy Rocks and Halterem's Loup before reaching the outskirts of St Abbs. The village and its headland are named for St Ebba, a 7th century priestess who founded a religious settlement in the area.

Walk down to the harbour, usually busy with small boats, and take the path climbing to the upper houses (passing public toilets). Walk along through the houses to reach the tarmac path leading round to Coldingham Bay, a fine sweep of sand popular with holidaymakers in summer. There are toilets here also.

Walk round the bay just above the sand, cross Homeli Knoll and go down steps to cross Milldown Burn. From here to Eyemouth the path is waymarked. It crosses fields and descends to the stony Linkim Shore,

Coldingham Bay.

then goes up Fleurs Dean and continues across a number of fields. Between Coldingham Bay and Linkim Shore the coastal rocks show intense folding, banding and faults, caused by the unimaginable pressures of different strata coming together aeons ago.

At Killiedraught Bay, just before Eyemouth, walk out onto the point, the farthest bit of which delights in the name of Hairy Ness. It is a pleasure to be here at any time of year as the sea crashes onto the rocks below and the wind freshens the air. On this headland is Eyemouth Fort, dating back to the 17th century. Interpretive boards tell its history.

Walk into Eyemouth and make your way along the seafront to the harbour, the major fishing port in Berwickshire. There is always plenty of activity to interest you, and nearby you can buy superb fresh fish, or if you are hungry after your walk, delicious fish and chips to eat while waiting for the bus back to St Abbs.

St Abbs Harbour.

You should not leave before visiting the Eyemouth Museum, which shares the Auld Kirk building with the tourist information centre. It has much of interest including a wonderful tapestry sewn by local women depicting the disaster of October 1881, when in a great gale many boats were sunk and the town lost 129 men. The tapestry took two years to make and was unveiled at the centenary of the disaster in 1981.

Hairy Ness, Eyemouth

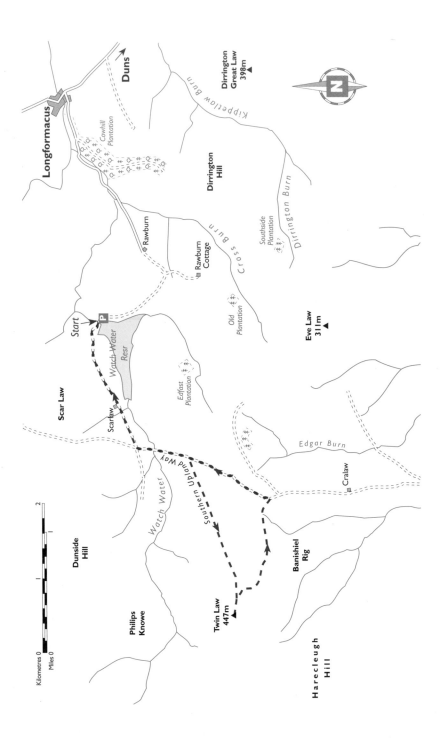

Longformacus

Duns

Cowhill Plantation

Dirrington Great Law 398m

Kippetlaw Burn

Dirrington Hill

Dirrington Burn

Rawburn

Cross Burn

Rawburn Cottage

Southside Plantation

Start

P

Watch Water Resr

Old Plantation

Eve Law 311m

Scar Law

Scarlaw

Edgst Plantation

Edgar Burn

Southern Upland Way

Cralaw

Dunside Hill

Watch Water

Banishiel Rig

Philips Knowe

Twin Law 447m

Harecleugh Hill

Kilometres 0   1   2
Miles 0   1

WATCH WATER AND TWIN LAW

One of the many advantages of walking in Scotland's border hills lies in the fact that the Southern Upland Way (SUW) passes through the region, wending its way eastward to its final destination at Cockburnspath, on Berwickshire's North Sea coast. This walk, which starts from the shores of the Watch Water reservoir, west of Longformacus, follows the SUW for some 4.5 km to reach the spectacular cairns on the summit of Twin Law.

From the parking area, walk south-west along the surfaced road to Scarlaw farm, cuddled in beside a shelter belt of mature beech and other hardwood trees. Beyond Scarlaw, at a crossroads, turn left and follow the SUW marker posts down to a ford and footbridge across the Watch Water. Look here for a memorial stone which sits above a well on the north bank of the stream. In bears the dates 1865 to 1897 and relates to a Rawburn keeper. The weathered inscription reads "There is no Water on the Lammermuirs sweeter than at John Dippie's Well". It still tastes sweet today!

Continue south along the broad track which is both SUW and Herring Road, the route used in olden times by country folk bringing home stocks of salted herring from Dunbar for winter use. Beyond a walled

Longformacus village.

John Dippie's Well.

Close-up of cairn on Twin Law hill.

plantation, at a gate, turn right beside a wire fence and follow the well defined path of the SUW as it heads up towards the summit of Twin Law. Near to the top, the fence meets a wall with a stile nearby. Cross over the stile and head directly towards the large stone cairns. These are the Twin Law Cairns which are such a prominent landmark throughout the Lammermuir Hills. The large barrel-shaped cairns rise out of two large piles of stones which may have been on this site since prehistoric times. Each of the cairns has a south facing seat recessed into it. From such a vantage point there are superb views of the Eildon Hills, the distant Cheviot Hills, and the nearby twin hills of Dirrington. There is usually a book kept in a tin box at the east cairn, in which passing walkers may enter their comments!

What of the history of the Twin Law Cairns? The original piles of stones are of great antiquity and may well have been gathered by early man to serve as burial or ceremonial cairns. The present well built cylinders are of comparatively recent date, the originals having been used for target practice by tanks training here during the Second World War. The legend of Twin Law is contained in an old border ballad "The Ballad of Twin Law". It relates how Scots and Saxon armies met at this place. They sent out their champions to do battle, not knowing they were brothers who had been parted in youth. They both died in mortal combat,

> "And they biggit twa cairns on the heather
> They biggit them round and high
> And they stand on the Twinlaw hill
> Where they twa brithers lie."

Nothing is certain however, and one version of the legend is as good as another. The cairns were rebuilt and the stone seats renewed in 1994.

From the cairns, retrace your steps towards the stile which you crossed on the way up. Some 200 m before the stile, follow a clear path which forks right, through the heather. The path skirts round an old quarry and continues to another fork. Take the left hand path which leads down a rough track by a young plantation, to reach a small gate in a wall. Beyond the gate follow an obvious vehicle track which meanders down through grass and heather to meet the main track coming up from Wedderlie. Turn left and walk along the track to reach the ford and bridge at the Watch Water. At cross tracks, turn right for Scarlaw and the Watch Water Reservoir.

Watch Water Reservoir.

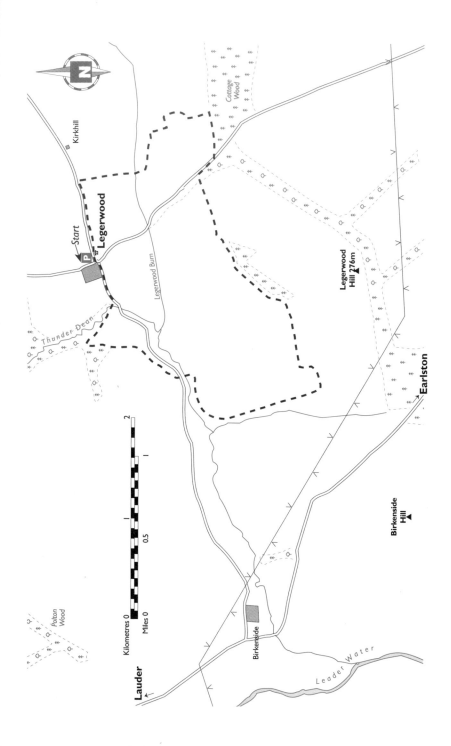

THE LEGERWOOD TRAIL

Legerwood farm nestles in the vale of Lauderdale midway between the higher "sheep hills" of the Southern Uplands to the west, and the lower fertile arable lands of the Merse further east. At an altitude of 171 m, Legerwood lies on the very southern edge of the Lammermuirs.

The farm is 1586 acres in size, and the trail was made possible with the active support of the Scott Aiton family who farm Legerwood. Bear in mind that this is a working farm, and in addition to following the country code, there are a couple of especially important points to remember. Don't touch or interfere with any farm machinery, and leave all livestock completely alone. It is not possible to take dogs on the trail. If you leave a dog in your car please do remember to leave a window slightly open, and in strong sunlight try to create some shade with a rug or towel.

There is an information board in the car park showing the route to be followed, together with up-to-date details of the walk, provided by the ranger service. There are also information sheets available from a leaflet dispenser in the car park.

From the car park walk down the tarmac road to the crossroads. Climb over the ladder stile at the telephone box, and follow the path up the left-hand side of the field. At the top of the field turn right and

INFORMATION

Distance: 4 km (2.5 miles).

Map: OS Landranger, sheet 73.

Start and finish: The car park at Legerwood, GR587433. Legerwood is signposted from the A68 and from the A6105 between Earlston and Gordon.

Terrain: Field paths and country lane. Quite a number of easy stiles. Boots or wellies recommended in wet weather.

Refreshments: None en route. Ample facilities in Lauder; Rhymers Tower Cafe beside the filling station in Earlston also recommended.

Public transport: Lowland Service 29 and 30 to and from Edinburgh along the A68. Phone Traveline on (0131) 225 3858 for details.

Note: This walk is particularly suitable for families with children. Note that the trail is open from 1 June to 30 September, 1000–1900 daily.

Legerwood Trail logo.

walk down to a footbridge over the ditch at the bottom of the field. Cross the footbridge and stile, turn left over another stile, following the track along the edge of the wood to its end. There is a lot of wildlife to be seen along this stretch of the trail. The ditch hosts a large variety of wild flowers and insects, while further east lies Everett Moss. This area of wetland is an important habitat for wildfowl. Mallard, teal and wading birds such as curlew, find plenty of feeding among the reedy marsh vegetation and its rich insect population.

On the Legerwood Trail.

After crossing a stile out of the wood, turn right and follow the edge of the field up and round to a stile leading on to a farm track. From this path Everett Moss can be seen in its entirety. At the eastern end of the moss are the remains of Corsbie Tower. This 15th century fortified house, inhabited by the Cranstouns of Corsbie, would have provided sanctuary during many a Border raid.

At the end of the farm track turn right on to the tarmac road. Turn right at the junction, and then left into woodland. Climb the stile ahead, turn right, and follow the track to a stile on the right. Once over the stile, turn left, and follow the conifer shelter belt out onto the hill. Do make sure to close the gate here. Sitka spruce and larch make up this shelter belt which is home to pigeons and rabbits. If you are very quiet, and very lucky, you may see a fox in this area.

In case of emergency, or if you wish to shorten the walk, turn right after the field gate and head downhill to a second field gate leading onto a track. Walk through the sheep pens, cross the stream and turn right along the tarmac road back to the car park.

To continue along the trail, walk up to the top of the hill for the best view over the farm. Return to the end of the conifer shelter belt and follow the fence down to a stile on the left. Climb the stile, and the stile at the water trough, before following the fence beside a newly planted wood to arrive at a field gate on the right.

Pass through the gate and follow the waymarked trail downhill by field and gate to reach the tarmac road. Note on the way down the rough ground on the left, and also the "hunt gates" set in fences to allow for the easy passage of mounted followers of the local hunt. Lower down, large beech trees are a feature of this part of the farm trail.

Cross the road with care, and climb over the stile opposite. Turn right and follow the field edge, firstly parallel to the road, and then uphill beside a cottage garden to arrive at the tree nursery. This enterprise produces some 50,000 native hardwoods and hedging plants, most of which are grown from locally collected seeds.

Walk through the nursery and leave it by crossing yet another stile. Turn right and follow the track round and down to the main road. Walk past the old smithy and the schoolhouse, to the bridge. Turn left and walk up to the car park.

If you have enjoyed this walk, come again in a different season, and see how much can change, say between early summer and late autumn. If you have any comment to make, please contact the Borders Regional Council Ranger Service, Harestanes Countryside Visitor Centre, Ancrum, Jedburgh TD8 6UQ (01835 830281), or leave a note in the honesty box at the car park.

Stile on the Legerwood Trail.

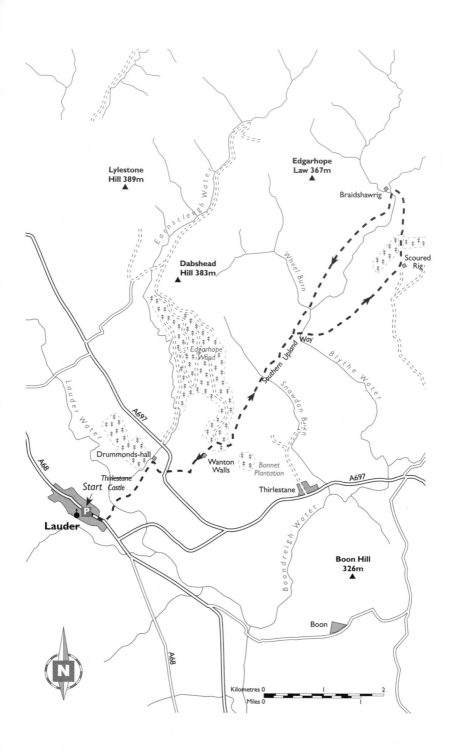

LAUDER AND BRAIDSHAWRIG

This longer walk in the south-west corner of the Lammermuir Hills starts and finishes in the border town of Lauder. It visits remote and abandoned farmsteads and is the very essence of these quiet and lonely hills.

Lauder has a Royal Charter dating from at least 1502, granted by King James IV. Prior to Scottish local government reorganisation in the mid 1970s, Lauder was the only Ancient and Royal Burgh in the county of Berwickshire. The old tolbooth which stands in the centre of the village is said to have been on its present site since the 14th century. It has been rebuilt on a number of occasions, always allegedly to its original design. Behind the tolbooth stands the unusual 17th century parish church. Centrally planned, a Greek cross with four equal arms sur-mounted by an octagonal bell tower, it was designed by Sir William Bruce for the Duke of Lauderdale of nearby Thirlestane Castle.

The old tolbooth in Lauder.

Lauder, like many a border town, has its own unique version of "Common Riding". The festivities begin on the first Saturday in August when the Cornet, the principal participant, leads over 300 riders to visit cairns marking out the town's historical common land.

Walk south along the A68, with the estate walls of Thirlestane Castle on your left. At the lodge, turn left, and walk down past the stable block. You are now on the Southern Upland Way. Follow the waymarked path and cross the Leader Water by a concrete bridge.

INFORMATION

Distance: 14.5 km (9 miles).

Map: OS Landranger, sheet 73.

Start and finish: Lauder, in the main street next to the Tolbooth.

Terrain: Field paths and moorland tracks. Boots recommended.

Refreshments: None en route. Hotels, pubs and chip shop in Lauder.

Public transport: Regular bus service to and from Edinburgh and the main Border towns.

Points of Interest: Thirlestane Castle at Lauder is one of the oldest and finest castles in Scotland. Famed for its magnificent state rooms and family nurseries, there is much more to see at Thirlestane than in many historic homes. Open at Easter and from May to September 1400 to 1700 (closed Saturdays). Phone 01578 722430 for details.

Thirlestane Castle near Lauder.

Turn right along the east bank of the river and at an old iron bridge turn right, away from the water, and follow the clear track up through field and woodland to the A697 Carfraemill to Greenlaw road. Cross the busy road with care and walk up to the farm of Wanton Walls. Follow the road left through the farm and up past the white painted water board pumping station.

Beyond an iron gate the track crosses an open field before entering a plantation by a 'new' stile. In this part of the walk concrete steps are now set into the wall to the side of gates. Together with a sturdy hand post they are easy to cross. Follow the SUW markers through the south-east corner of Edgarhope Wood. As the path comes out of the wood turn left, over a stile and into a grass field. Bear left uphill and, following the wall on your left, head for a wooden stile at the edge of the wood. Over the stile bear right and follow the SUW marker posts over the hill and down to the Snawdon Burn. Across the burn turn left, and in about 150 m cross yet another stile and turn right.

The 'Way' now climbs out onto the open moor, the real start of the Lammermuir Hills. This is sheep country with wide views beneath a big sky. Hear, according to season, the sound of skylark, curlew, grouse and lapwing. Away to the north-east two pimples on the horizon are the Twinlaw Cairns above Watch Water Reservoir (Walk 7). To the south are the Eildon Hills, and further south the Cheviots.

Follow the SUW waymarkers down to near the point where the Wheel Burn meets the Blythe Water. Cross the Blythe Water by a substantial footbridge to the east bank, and climb the ridge ahead to reach a gateway in a wall with an adjacent stile. Once on the crest of the ridge the Way follows a fence along Scoured Rig. The path leads to a track heading northwards into a rectangular plantation. Follow the path down through the plantation to emerge on the hillside above the empty farm buildings of Braidshawrig. It must have been a lonely life for those who lived here in the past. Tracks lead off from Braidshawrig to Bermuda and to Sebastapol, exotic names indeed for such remote and isolated places!

Bridge taking the Southern Upland Way over the Blythe Water.

Walk down to the farm building and cross to the west bank of the Blythe Water at any convenient spot. A clear track heads in a southerly direction away from Braidshawrig, initially keeping close to Blythe Water. A standing stone, between the boundary wall and the burn, commemorates the 12th Earl of Lauderdale who was killed by lightning here in 1884.

Stride out in a south westerly direction for some 2 km, along a well defined track, to rejoin the SUW near the junction of the Wheel Burn and the Blythe Water. This track is a variation of the Herring Road by which monks and country people brought salted herring from Dunbar to the Abbeys and villages of the borders.

Retrace your steps to Lauder by following again the marker posts of the SUW, across the Snawdon Burn, uphill to the plantation and down to Wanton Walls. Re-cross the A697 and walk down through the policies of Thirlestane Castle. Cutting across the last field, the oldest part of the castle can be seen to advantage. The original building was commissioned in the 16th century by John Maitland, Chancellor of Scotland. In the 17th and 19th centuries, additions were made to the front of the building by the Dukes of Lauderdale.

The castle, which has 98 rooms, is open to the public (see Information) and contains the Border Museum of Country Life. It is well worth a visit.

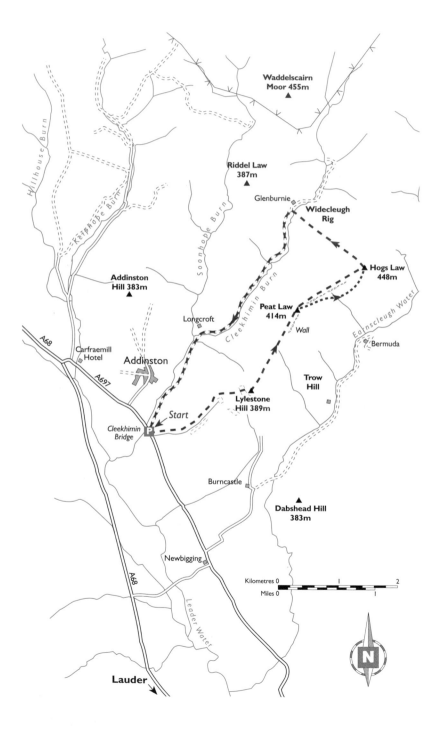

LAMMERMUIR RIDGE WALK

This is a pleasant ridge walk in the south-west corner of the Lammermuir Hills. It visits three named hill tops and returns down a typical Lammermuir valley.

Cleekhimin Bridge is on the A697, 1.5 km south-east of its junction with the A68 and the Carfraemill Hotel. This popular meeting place was originally an 18th century posting inn. It was extended and modernised in the 1930s and many Art Deco features remain from that period.

The bridge at Cleekhimin may not be one of the Borders' most spectacular river crossings, but a plaque on the the south parapet states that the original bridge was built in 1758. It was destroyed by floods and rebuilt in 1892. It was again rebuilt to new levels in 1961 by the then Berwickshire County Council. Rodgers of nearby Earlston were the contractors both in 1892 and 1961.

If travelling from the direction of the A68 (Edinburgh 37 km) turn left into the minor road leading to Longcroft Farm. Park on the grass verge at any convenient spot along this road near to its junction with the A697. There is a building on either side of the junction, the older building was the local school and the other is a modern bungalow.

Walk back to the main road and turn left. Turn left again and go through a gate at the side of the new

INFORMATION

Distance: 11.5 km (7 miles).

Map: OS Landranger, sheet 73.

Start and finish: Cleekhimin Bridge on A697.

Terrain: Easy walking over grazing land, open moor and farm tracks. Strong footwear advised.

Refreshments: None on route. Bar meals, tasty sandwiches and good beer available at nearby Carfraemill Hotel. Ample facilities in Lauder.

Public transport: Regular bus service down A68.

Carfraemill Hotel.

property. Walk up the right-hand edge of the field, keeping to the left of a burn. At the top of the field, go through a metal gate and head uphill, walking to the left of a tree-lined gully. Near the top of the gully pass through an old wooden gate and, leaving the trees behind, walk uphill making for an old plantation not marked on the Landranger map.

At the plantation go through an old wooden gate (or what's left of it!) and head up the left-hand edge of the wood. Beyond the trees go up the hillside, heading slightly to the right, to reach the shelter belt of trees crowning the summit of Lylestone Hill (389 m). The windswept mixture of pine and hardwood trees is bounded on the north-east side by a broken stone wall.

From Lylestone Hill head NNE over open grassland for about 250 m to reach a green metal gate at a junction between a wire fence and the end of an old stone wall. Go through the gate, and keeping the wall on your left, walk the 1.5 km to the 414 m top of Peat Law. Along this direct route there are a couple of muddy patches where cattle have been and there is an

New fence running between the old drystane dyke and the track.

old wire fence to cross. Watch out also for remnants of rusty fencing wire in the grass near the wall, the fence on the other side having been recently renewed.

When the rather dilapidated stone wall reaches the summit of Peat Law there is a choice of routes to the next objective, the 448 m top of Hogs Law. Either climb over a rusty old iron gate and continue beside the friendly old wall, or climb over the same gate, turn right through a newer gate, and then left along a clear broad track through the heather. The wall bends slightly right here and then heads directly for Hogs Law some 1.25 km distant.

If you have elected to follow the wall towards Hogs Law note that it ends halfway up the hill, and you will only have the new wire fence for company

The track through the heather bends away from the fence/wall for some distance but bends back again to meet the fence at the summit cairn – a somewhat untidy pile of stones.

Here is typical Lammermuir country with big skies and wide horizons. The haunting cry of curlew, the startled call of peewits and oyster catchers and the liquid song of the skylark are all heard according to season. On a warm day in summer 1994 the author watched a pair of buzzards soaring high above Hogs Law. Their "mewing" was the only sound that broke the silence.

Whichever option has been taken to reach the summit of Hogs Law, the route makes a change of

A typical Sheepfold found in the Border Hills.

direction here. There is an older wire fence leading away from the cairned top and heading in an north-westerly direction down Widecleugh Rig. After passing through a gate, and keeping the fence on your left, follow it all the way downhill to the abandoned farm buildings of Glenburnie above the Whalplaw Burn. The fence drops down steeply towards the river, so do take extra care.

Cross the water at any convenient spot to reach the well defined track on the west bank. Turn left here and follow the "road" beside the tumbling burn for some 3 km down to the cottages of Longcroft. The attractive farmhouse is hidden in trees on the right. Go through a final gate out onto the tarmac, bear left and walk down the single track road beside the Cleekhimin Burn to Cleekhimin Bridge.

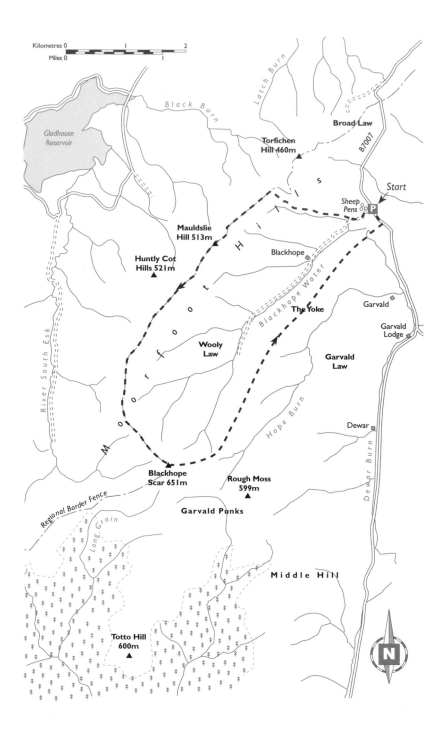

BLACKHOPE SCAR

Generally speaking, the Moorfoot Hills are less interesting and wetter underfoot in the north and east of the range. The higher, drier, and more prominent hills, lie mainly in the south and west of this upland area. Blackhope Scar lies somewhere in between.

At 651 m Blackhope Scar is the highest point in Midlothian and can only be reached by a fairly long and sometimes tedious walk. The walk to the summit described here, although long, has a couple of advantages over other routes. Firstly there is the security of a fence for almost the entire way, making navigation in poor weather conditions simplicity itself. Secondly, for a considerable distance in its early stages, the walk follows the north-western ridge of the Moorfoot escarpment. The views on a clear, fine day from Mauldslie Hill are quite spectacular.

To reach the start turn off the A7 Edinburgh to Galashiels road at Middleton onto the B7007 road to

INFORMATION

Distance: 20 km (12.5 miles).

Map: OS Landranger, sheet 73.

Start and finish: On B7007 near access road to Blackhope Farm.

Terrain: Moorland tracks which can be wet underfoot in winter months. Boots or strong shoes advised.

Refreshments: None en route.

Public transport: None.

Hay shed by Blackhope Farm.

Innerleithen. After climbing up the escarpment edge
the road takes a left turn into the hills. Beyond a
cutting, the access road to Blackhope Farm will be
found on the right. A car can be parked on the grass
verge near to the farm road end but do look out for
ditches! Permission may be given by asking at the
farm, to park off the road near to wooden sheep pens
just inside the farm road. The shepherd's cottage is the
one on the right just beyond the big new sheds, and
before the main farmhouse.

Having parked your car, walk down the farm road to a
hairpin bend near to a tall and rather unusual hay
shed. Turn right off the road, scramble up an eroded
bank, and walk up a well defined path to the right of a
hill burn. The gently rising path heads up a shallow
valley which appears to be little grazed by the hill
sheep. Down by the burn, rushes and bog cotton grow,
while in the damp ground nearby, marsh orchids may
be found. Nearer to the path tall and slender thistles
abound. There are other wild flowers by the wayside
which enthusiastic botanists will be able to identify.

As the path heads up towards a col, it passes to the
right of an old stone sheep pen before arriving at a
wooden gate in a wire fence. The path beyond the gate
leads down to Mauldslie, a farm near the south-eastern
shore of Gladhouse Reservoir. This route however
does not pass through the gate but turns up left beside
the wire fence. The fence marks the boundary
between Lothian and Borders Regions, and will be
followed for the next 6 km to the summit of
Blackhope Scar.

Follow the faint vehicle tracks uphill beside the fence
heading in the first instance for the 513 m top of
Mauldslie Hill. It is here that you will be pleased to
have picked a dry clear day for this particular walk. In
the foreground can be seen Gladhouse Reservoir with
the outline of the Pentland Hills beyond. Further right
Salisbury Crags (spelt Craigs on OS maps) and
Arthur's Seat above the City of Edinburgh are clearly
seen.

Further right again can be seen the twin chimney stacks of Cockenzie power station, followed by North Berwick Law, and almost in line with the fence the unmistakable outline of Traprain Law. The islands of the Forth, Inchcolm, Inchmickery and Inchkeith may be pinpointed, together with the coast and hills of Fife. On a really clear day the Grampian Mountains and Lochnagar can be seen almost 160 km to the north.

As the fence swings left in a more southerly direction, it has recently been renewed. Care must be taken here as old posts and some rusty wires have been left behind. It is surprising that the vehicles which bring up new posts and wire don't always seem to take away the old material, not only here but elsewhere as well. The final stretch to the summit heads south-east and it is here in wet weather that the worst of the boggy gullies are to be found and negotiated.

Stand at last by the trig point, and hills and rolling moorland will be seen in every direction. The 622 m summit of Dundreich is just 4 km to the west, while Dunslair Heights and Glentress Forest lie to the south. Looking east, the moorland of Ladyside Heights, Deaf Heights and Windlestraw Law fill the skyline.

Start the return journey by heading east by a fence which soon swings in a north-easterly direction. This is also boggy ground which makes for slow progress. You may need to cross or re-cross the fence to find the easiest ground. Keep walking down the ridge, which is parallel to, but slightly lower than, the ascending ridge.

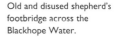
Old and disused shepherd's footbridge across the Blackhope Water.

Follow the fence downhill, over The Yoke and over a final hill to the east of Blackhope Farm. Leave the fence at last and ford the Blackhope Water. On the far bank either bear right and follow a fence uphill to a gate at the main road, or turn left and follow a farm track which leads to the farm road below the conspicuous hay shed.

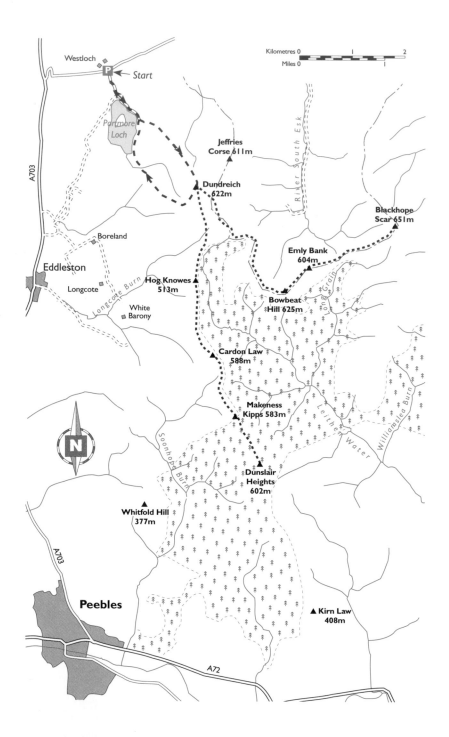

DUNDREICH FROM PORTMORE LOCH

The summit of Dundreich (622 m) marks the highest point in the north-west corner of the Moorfoot Hills. The area of high ground generally known as Jeffries Corse is prominent to the east of the A703, midway between Leadburn crossroads and the popular town of Peebles.

To reach the start, turn east off the A703, 10 km north of Peebles, onto the unclassified road signposted "Temple". In 1.3 km there is parking available on the right hand side of the road near the junction with the access road to Portmore Loch. Leave the car in the lay-by and head up the gravel track towards the loch. Please take note of the sign which forbids dogs to be taken along this route.

On reaching the dam end (in 800 m) turn left, and after crossing a bridge over the Loch Burn, go through the large metal gate ahead. A sign on the gate states "Please Keep To The Track" with an arrow pointing forward. Beyond the gate turn sharp right and follow a wide track along and above the east shore of Portmore.

The loch used to supply water to top up the nearby Gladhouse Reservoir and to supply the needs of the farm at Westloch. The water is now well stocked with fish and is a mecca for local angling enthusiasts.

Continue walking along the track, and after passing through a second metal gate, arrive at a wooden gate near to a conifer plantation. Do not go through this wooden gate but head up left towards an obvious path which leads to the wall bordering the plantation. Climb uphill beside the wall, which eventually disappears into the wood and is replaced by a wire fence.

At the top of the plantation rejoin the wall (and fence), and after first dropping down to a shallow saddle, climb steadily up beside wall and fence to reach

INFORMATION

Distance: 8 km (5 miles).

Map: OS Landranger, sheet 73.

Start and finish: Gravel lay-by on roadside at the junction with the access road to Portmore Loch at GR256514.

Terrain: Good tracks and hill paths throughout. Some steep sections up towards the summit. Boots and strong shoes advised.

Refreshments: None en route.

Public transport: Bus service between Edinburgh and Peebles down the A703 (1.3 km west of start).

Note: Dogs are not allowed along this route under any circumstances.

the top of Dundreich. Near the top, the wall ends at a junction with a netting fence. Cross over the wall and make for the nearby summit trig point.

The views from the rounded top are wide and distant in all directions. Some 4 km to the east lies the high ground of Blackhope Scar (Walk 11), while to the south can be seen the radio masts atop Dunslair Heights (Walk 13). The Pentland Hills are prominent to the north-west, and to the north can be seen the Edinburgh Hills and over the Forth beyond.

Leave the summit and head south-west along the wide ridge following a distinct vehicle track through the grass. At a fork take the right-hand track and soon bear right again to walk down a narrow ridge to a rocky promontory. With Portmore Loch in sight, head steeply down between crags to reach the valley floor.

An easier if slightly longer descent may be made by following a faint vehicle track down the right shoulder of the hill. This track then bears left to join the path coming down from the rough ground above. When an obvious farm track is met turn right and follow its route firstly across a stream, and then through a large gap in an old wall. Walk across the field ahead to reach a large tubular metal gate.

Beyond the gate bear right, and follow the broad track beside the loch shore. Pass through one wooden and two metal gates before turning right and heading back down the access road to your parked car.

Dundreich can also be climbed quite easily from Moorfoot Farm south of Gladhouse Reservoir. Beyond Gladhouse Cottage keep to the west bank of the South Esk and after crossing a couple of hill burns ascend a well defined ridge to the summit. Walkers wanting a longer expedition can, from Dundreich, follow the summit ridge and fence via Bowbeat Hill (625 m) and Emly Bank (604 m) to Blackhope Scar. A similar extended ridge walk may be had by walking south over Hog Knowes, Cardon Law and Makeness Kipps to Dunslair Heights.

Opposite: Going down the ridge towards Portmore Loch, with the Pentland Hills in the background.

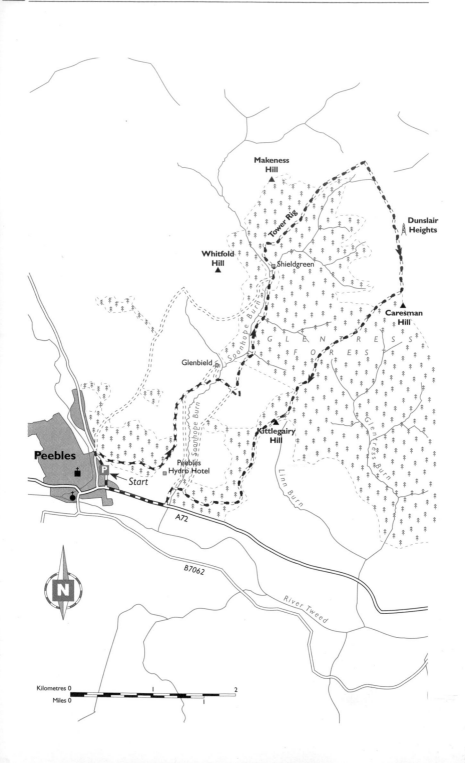

Makeness
Hill

Tower Rig

Dunslair
Heights

Whitfold
Hill

Shieldgreen

Caresman
Hill

G L E N T R E S S   F O R E S T

Glenbield

Kittlegairy
Hill

Peebles

Peebles
Hydro Hotel

P

Start

A72

B7062

River Tweed

N

Kilometres 0   1   2
Miles 0   1

DUNSLAIR HEIGHTS

Peebles, a bonny town on the River Tweed, marks the south-western limit of the Moorfoot Hills. Dunslair Heights (602 m) stand some 4.5 km north-east of the town and are a prominent Border landmark. The walker heading for the Heights has a choice of routes, which have as their first objective the white buildings of Shieldgreen Outdoor Centre.

From the car park, walk north along Edinburgh Road. Turn right along Venlaw High Road, and after about 300 m take the clear track on the left (Forestry Commission signboard). The track climbs steadily as it winds round the eastern side of Ven Law through mixed woodland, and then levels out to run above the valley of the Soonhope Burn. On the far side of the burn are a number of small wooden chalets used at weekends. The mast on Dunslair Heights is now clearly visible high to your right.

The path emerges from the wood at a pleasing sign welcoming you to walk in the area. In 400 m, with the farm of Glenbield clearly in view, go right at a "walking man" sign, steeply downhill then swinging

INFORMATION

Distance: 15 km (9 miles).

Start and finish: Large free car park in Edinburgh Road, Peebles, 300 m north of the A703/A72 junction.

Map: OS Landranger, sheet 73.

Terrain: Good paths and forest tracks. Some steep sections. Boots or strong shoes advised.

Refreshments: None en route. Facilities of all kinds in Peebles.

Public transport: Regular bus services to Peebles from Edinburgh and the other Border towns.

Shieldgreen in winter.

Shieldgreen with Dunslair
Heights beyond.

left by a fence. Join a track coming down from the
farm and cross the Soonhope Burn by a plank bridge.
Go uphill beside the fence to reach a broad track, and
turn left.

As you round a bend the white buildings of
Shieldgreen are clearly visible ahead. Re-enter the
forest at a gate and stile. In 200 m, fork left and then
continue along the main track for a kilometre to reach
Shieldgreen. A plaque on the front of the building
proclaims "Crookston Castle School Shieldgreen
Centre. Opened by Lord Taylor of Gryffe, Chairman
of the Forestry Commission, on Saturday 17th May
1975".

Turn right, up the track leading to the centre, and
follow a path up the left-hand side of outbuildings.
The path climbs steeply behind Shieldgreen to meet a
forestry road. Cross the road and walk up through the
trees to meet a second road. Follow the clear path
beyond the road as it climbs for 1 km up the open
hillside to reach a saddle north-west of Dunslair
Heights.

At the saddle turn right and walk up beside an old
fence to reach, in about 800 m, the radio masts and
meteorological station on the summit of Dunslair

Heights. Before getting there you may well have heard the wind whistling and humming through the wires of the masts. The views are extensive, particularly to the north and north-east over the Moorfoot Hills towards Dundreich (Walk 12) and Blackhope Scar (Walk 11). It will probably have taken you about two hours to reach this point.

The return route is through Glentress Forest. The forest is characterised by a multitude of forestry roads, tracks and paths, many of them dead ends. The description of the way down is therefore quite detailed and should be carefully followed. You should basically be heading downhill in a south-westerly direction for most of the way.

Leave the summit by a distinct track heading south. Where the track swings right through a fence, keep left to follow a path through grass, with a broken wall on the left and the forest edge on your right. Soon cross through the wall, turn right and continue, now with the broken wall on your right.

Where a new wall starts, close to a dark green marker post, turn right, down a track which is often muddy into the forest. The track soon meets a forestry road; turn left here and walk downhill for 2 km to a true T-junction, ignoring a track coming down from the right. At the T-junction turn right, and in 25 m arrive at another T-junction. Go straight ahead here on a clear footpath between the trees.

At a clearing, follow the path round left to meet yet another forest road. Turn right here, and walk downhill through the forest for a further 2 km, to a left-hand hairpin bend. A few paces beyond the bend, look for a steeply descending path on the right.

This path emerges on to the road opposite the goods entrance of the Peebles Hotel Hydro. Turn left along the road, then right along Innerleithen Road in front of the grounds of the impressive hotel. At the roundabout, turn right into Edinburgh Road and the car park.

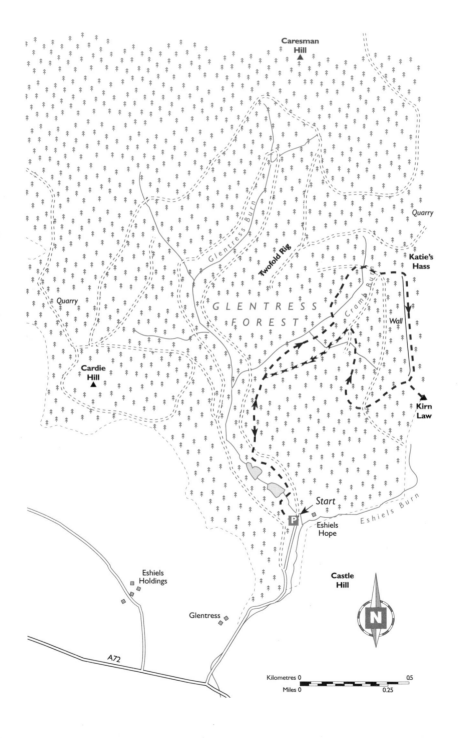

Caresman Hill

Quarry

Glentress Burn

Twofold Rig

Katie's Hass

Crams Burn

GLENTRESS FOREST

Quarry

Wall

Cardie Hill

Kirn Law

Start

Eshiels Burn

Eshiels Hope

Eshiels Holdings

Castle Hill

Glentress

N

A72

Kilometres 0 0.5
Miles 0 0.25

KIRN LAW

This is one of a number of waymarked routes through the forest of Glentress. The forest extends almost from the banks of the River Tweed to an elevation of just over 600 m. Glentress is the oldest of Forestry Commission forests in southern Scotland, with the earliest plantings having been made in 1920, just one year after the Commission was formed as a response to the timber crisis caused by the demands of the Great War.

Head east out of the busy town of Peebles on the A72 Galashiels road. In some 3 km turn left and follow the signs for Glentress Forest Park in the main Falla Brae car park with information boards and public toilets nearby. A study of the forest information boards will help you to select a suitable walk. Each walk is colour coded and graded easy, moderate or strenuous. The distance and time taken for each walk is also given.

It would be a good idea to pick up a copy of the free leaflet "Forests of the Tweed Valley" from either the Tourist Information Centre in Peebles High Street or the Forest Enterprise office at Greenside, Peebles, to take with you on your walk. The leaflets are often also available on site. The Kirn Law walk is 4.8 km long and could take up to two hours depending on the length of your picnic stop and time spent admiring the views.

A word about the waymarking on this walk may be helpful. On the leaflet it is shown in orange, but on the walk itself, while many of the waymarks are indeed banded orange, others are a more pinky colour, so don't worry if you see both – you are still on course.

Walk out of the car park, cross the forest road, and cut down right beside the toilet block. The path soon passes to the right of a couple of attractive ponds. Created some years ago, these ponds now form an interesting habitat in their own right. They are home to fish, duck and other wildlife. You may even spot a heron standing by the water's edge.

INFORMATION

Distance: 5 km (3 miles).

Map: OS Landranger, sheet 73.

Start and finish: Falla Brae car park in Glentress. This is the main forest car park.

Terrain: Forest tracks and paths throughout. No special footwear needed.

Refreshments: None en route. Take a picnic. Ample facilities in Peebles or Innerleithen.

Public transport: Regular bus service to nearby Peebles from Edinburgh and other border towns.

Forest trail to Kirn Law.

One of the ponds in
Glentress Forest.

Near to the second pond, the path cuts up to the right
to meet another forest road. Turn left here, and in
50 m, follow a path into the forest on the right. Walk
up through the trees for five minutes or so before
dropping down to regain the forest road. Turn right
and in 75 m go left on a path.

The path winds around through the trees (mostly
fairly dense spruce) and goes downhill briefly before
climbing again. At the top of a series of zig-zags turn
right on a track, and at a T-junction in 250 m turn
right again on a forest road. At the next right-hand
bend, go left on a path (watch carefully for the
waymark) that goes steeply uphill.

At a junction of paths, go right, through a gap in the
wall, and right again to walk uphill beside the wall,
following the path to the viewpoint on Kirn Law, at a
wall junction. In clear weather there are excellent
views from here down the Tweed Valley towards
Innerleithen, and across to the forest of Cardrona. The
prominent outline of Lee Pen (502 m) is seen to
advantage to the south-east. A very fine viewpoint, it
can be climbed easily from Innerleithen by gaining the
ridge between an ancient fort and St Ronan's Well.

To the right of the viewpoint, near where a wire fence meets the old wall, follow the markers into the wood. In a few paces, turn right and walk downhill on a distinct path through mature woodland to meet a broader path. Turn left and follow this path down to a main forest track, near to a picnic seat commanding good views up the valley to Peebles.

Turn left and almost immediately cut down to the right on a sometimes steep and narrow path. Briefly join a track, and then at the main forest road turn left, and retrace your steps downhill to the ponds, to return to the Falla Brae car park.

Similar walking routes can be followed in Cardrona Forest and Yair Forest, both of which lie on the south side of the River Tweed. Those with an interest in wildlife will find that the Tweed Valley forests have much to offer the quiet walker. Roe deer are plentiful and red squirrels, badgers and foxes are present.

Some 80 species of birds have been recorded in and around the forest areas, and bird and bat boxes have been provided in selected parts of the forest. At the present time about one third of land growing trees in the Borders is managed by Forest Enterprise, part of the Forestry Commission.

Another of the attractive ponds in Glentress Forest.

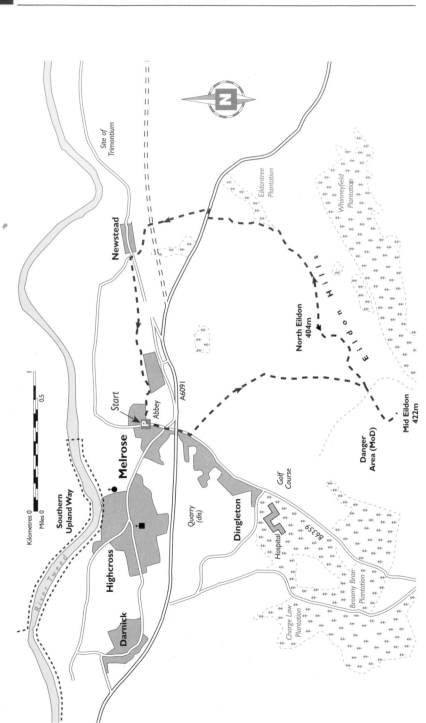

Site of Trimontium

Newstead

Eildontree Plantation

Whinneyfield Plantation

Eildon Hills

North Eildon 404m

Mid Eildon 422m

Danger Area (MoD)

A6091

Start

Abbey

P

Melrose

Southern Upland Way

Kilometres 0
Miles 0
0.5

River Tweed

Highcross

Darnick

Quarry (dis)

Dingleton

Golf Course

Hospital

B6359

Broomy Brae Plantation

Charge Law Plantation

THE EILDON HILLS

Although they are of only modest height, no book of walks in the Border Hills would be complete without the inclusion of the Eildons. From almost every vantage point throughout the Lammermuir, Moorfoot, or Tweedsmuir Hills, the prominent outline of these heather clad hills is in view. Whether from close to, or from far away, their distinctive shape is a friendly landmark and point of reference. Situated south of the historic Border town of Melrose, the Eildon Hills rise up out of a relatively lowland area, west of an attractive loop of the River Tweed.

Perhaps no other group of hills are soaked in as much myth, legend, folk lore, and history as the Eildons. They were formed, it is said, by Michael Scott the Wizard, commanding the Devil to split a single mountain into three. Michael Scott is supposedly buried in Melrose Abbey.

INFORMATION

Distance: 8 km (5 miles).

Map: OS Landranger, sheet 73.

Start and finish: Melrose market square by the B6359 Lilliesleaf road.

Car park: In the main car park near Melrose Abbey.

Terrain: Good hill tracks and minor roads. Boots or strong shoes advised.

Refreshments: Ample hotels, youth hostels, cafes and pubs in Melrose.

Public transport: Bus services to/from other Border towns and Edinburgh.

Points of Interest: Visit the ruins of 12th century Melrose Abbey, considered by many to be the most beautiful of all the Border abbeys. Beneath the chancel is said to lie the heart of Robert the Bruce. Open 0930 to 1800 Monday to Saturday, and 1400 to 1800 on Sundays. Next door to the Abbey, the National Trust for Scotland's Priorwood garden is also worth a visit.

Melrose Abbey.

Thomas Learmont, known also at Thomas the Rhymer, the 13th century Scottish bard and prophet, was spirited away by the fairies from under the Eildon tree. He spent seven years in the service of the Queen of Elfland beneath the Eildon Hills.

On his return he is said to have been able to foretell the future, one of his best known predictions being:

> "When Tweed and Powsail meet at Merlin's grave, Scotland and England shall one monarch have."

A saying said to have been literally fulfilled on the day when James VI of Scotland was crowned king of the united realms. Merlin's grave is said to lie close to Drumelzier Church (see Walk 17).

Everyone knows of course, that King Arthur sleeps with his army of knights in the deep recesses of the Eildons, ready when the need arises, to spring to the defence of the nation!

So much for the myth, legend and folklore, now for the facts. The Eildon Hills were formed as a result of

Leaderfoot Viaduct can be seen from the Eildon Hills.

activity beneath the earths crust some 350 million years ago, and now only exposed in their present shape after millions of years of weathering and glacial activity. No wizardry, just geological evolution.

Over 2,000 years ago North Hill was the site of a veritable city, the headquarters of the Selgovae tribe. Some 300 hut circles have been identified, suggesting a population of over 2,000. Such a society must have been involved in trade, localised industry, and agriculture on a considerable scale. The Selgovae fort was established on a site first inhabited by man as early as the 6th/7th century BC.

Then came the Romans. In the 1st century AD they swept north over the Cheviot Hills, displaced the Selgovae and built a signal station in the middle of their fort. This communication centre served the Roman road of Dere Street and the nearby Roman camp of Trimontium for perhaps 300 years.

In the recent past there has been yet another military development. The Ministry of Defence has extended

its activities into the Eildons. Red and white post and notices surrounding Mid Hill, serve to keep walkers off the hill when firing is taking place on the range below. Nowadays the firing only rarely interferes with access. Details of when the range is in use can be obtained from Melrose Tourist Information Centre.

The Eildon Hills from the south.

The Eildons will forever be romantically linked with Sir Walter Scott (1771–1832), Scottish poet and novelist, who made his home at Abbotsford House 4 km west of Melrose, close to the River Tweed. One of the poet's favourite views, now known as Scott's View, was from Bemersyde Hill just 4 km east of Melrose. This outstanding vista looks across the Tweed to the Eildon Hills beyond. Scott is buried in St Mary's Aisle, among the ruins of nearby Dryburgh Abbey.

This walk to the Eildon Hills start directly from Melrose. Park in the large car park near to the Abbey and walk up to the town square. Leave the square by the B6359 Lilliesleaf road, and turn left between houses where a sign indicates "Eildon Walk". Climb the steps behind the buildings and follow the clear path over fields and stiles to the lower slopes of the hills.

Beyond the last field bear right and follow the path as is traverses the hillside, through an expanse of gorse, towards the saddle between North and Mid Hills. At the saddle, turn right and head up the steep path to the summit of Mid Hill.

There is a view indicator here, erected by public subscription to the memory of Sir Walter Scott, who was "wont to view and point the glories of the Borderland" from this spot. Needless to say the views from Mid Hill are truly panoramic.

Return to the saddle, taking care coming down off Mid Hill as the scree can be loose underfoot. From the saddle walk up the broad track onto the 404 m summit of North Hill. It is here that early man, the Selgovae, and the Romans have left their mark.

To return to Melrose leave the summit in a north-easterly direction. Where the path divides, take the left hand branch, and descend with care (it is quite steep) down to the corner of a small wood. Cross over a stile and walk down a track which is often muddy, to the main road. Turn right along the main road and in a few metres turn left and walk down a signposted track. An underpass takes you across the new bypass from Melrose to the A68.

Go under the railway bridge and immediately turn left following the track to the west end of Newstead. Cross the road and head towards some stables. Pass through a gate between the stables and a row of houses. Walk along the narrow path behind the houses and along the embankment into Priorswalk housing estate.

At a gap in the houses, bear right, and follow the path over a bridge and through the park next to Melrose Abbey. At the National Trust for Scotland shop, turn left for Melrose Square, or right for the car park.

If time allows either before or after the walk, do make a special effort to visit the ruins of the 12th century Melrose Abbey, often considered to be the most beautiful of the Border Abbeys. Beneath the chancel is said to lie the heart of Robert the Bruce. Next door to it, the National Trust for Scotland's Priorwood Garden is also well worth a visit.

Having completed this walk you will have sampled the very stuff of which Border legend and history is made.

Mid Eildon.

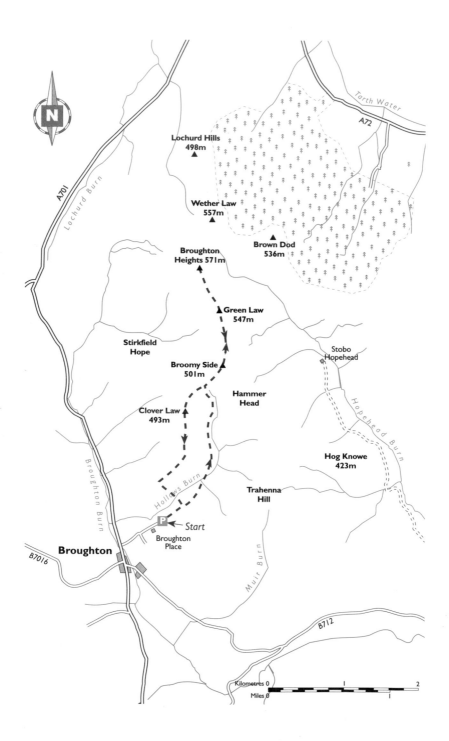

BROUGHTON HEIGHTS

Broughton Heights, in Tweeddale, are in the north-west corner of the Tweedsmuir Hills area, near to the junction of the A701 and the A72. This walk starts from just north of the village of Broughton, climbs up to the top of Broomy Side and along the ridge by way of Green Law, to the summit and trig point of Broughton Heights (571 m). The return can easily be made over the top of Clover Law.

Broughton lies on the A701 some 43 km south of Edinburgh. Just north of the village, and at GR611369, turn up the access road leading to Broughton Place Farm. There is also a sign at the main

INFORMATION

Distance: 10 km (6 miles).

Map: OS Landranger, sheet 72.

Start and finish: Broughton Place. On grass near shepherd's cottage. Boots or strong shoes essential.

Terrain: Good hill tracks and grassy tops.

Refreshments: None en route. Hotel and cafe in Broughton. Ample facilities in nearby Biggar.

Public transport: Minimal service along A701. Limited service Peebles to Biggar.

Looking west towards Broughton Place.

road pointing the way to Broughton Gallery. Drive up the road, pass the farm buildings, and park either in front of the castle-like building which houses the gallery, or on grass further along the track towards a shepherd's cottage.

Walk through the gate to the right of the cottage and head up the broad grass track ahead. Beyond a small plantation the track descends towards the Hollows Burn. Cross the stream and walk up a clear path through heather. The path continues up into a shallow valley, and crosses the somewhat muddy upper reaches of the Hollows Burn. The obvious path now climbs up to a fence and a gate at the col between Clover Law and Broomy Side. The gate is hidden until the last few metres, but the path does lead directly to it.

Beyond the gate, the path turns sharp right and heads uphill, by the side of a rather dilapidated wire fence, to the top of Broomy Side. Continue now in a more northerly direction, and following the fence, walk over Green Law and on up to the trig point on Broughton Heights (571 m).

If you have picked a clear dry day for this outing, you will be well rewarded by the panoramic views from the summit. To the north-west the lovely Pentland Hills will be clearly seen, while to the north there are extensive views towards Edinburgh, and beyond.

To the west and south-west the hills roll away towards the Culter and Lowther Hills, with Tinto prominent beyond the youthful River Clyde. With compass and map in hand, you can spend some time picking out the numerous landmarks.

Hollows Burn.

To make an alternative return, retrace your footsteps to the col between Broomy Side and Clover Law. Follow a distinct track beside the wire fence up onto the summit of Clover Law. Follow the grassy ridge in a southerly and then south-westerly direction. Near the end of the ridge, leave the fence and cut down left to cross the Hollows Burn between the trees and the shepherd's cottage. Regain the track, turn right, and head down the path to your waiting car.

A longer excursion may be made in the area by following the outward route, but climbing up to the col between Broomy Side and Hammer Head. Pass through a gate, and keeping right at a fork, head east on the old drove road over the shoulder of Hammer Head. Drop down to the Stobo Hopehead road, turn right and follow the road down through the policies of Stobo Castle to the B712.

Turn right along the road and in 2 km, just before crossing the River Tweed, go through a metal gate and follow a track down by the river. Cut up right onto the track bed of the disused railway line and follow it, for some 5 km, all the way back to Broughton village. A further 2 km will return you to Broughton Place.

Broughton Place.

John Buchan, the Scottish novelist, biographer, publisher, lawyer and diplomat (1875–1940) had long associations with the area. In the old Free Kirk at Broughton, where John Buchan's father came as a clergyman, a museum has been created by Biggar Museum Trust commemorating his life and achievements.

Buchan set many of his adventure novels in the area, and took the title Lord Tweedsmuir when elevated to the peerage. One of his best known novels, *Greenmantle*, published in 1916, lives on in the name of Greenmantle Ale brewed by Broughton Brewery Ltd, and the Greenmantle Hotel in Broughton village.

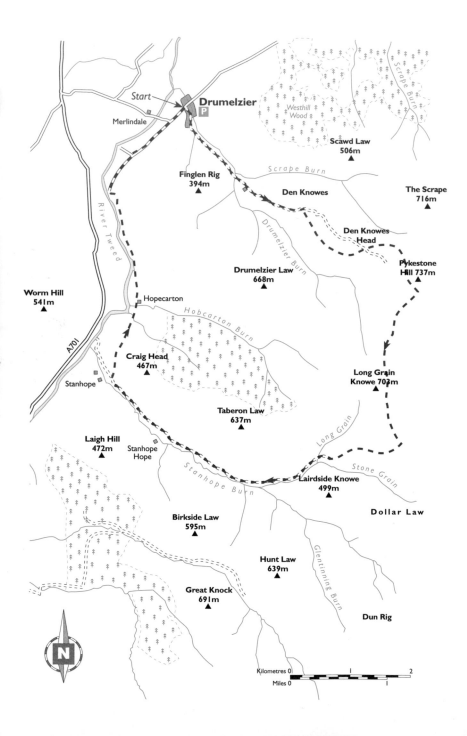

Start

Drumelzier

Merlindale

Westhill Wood

Scrape Burn

Scawd Law
506m

Finglen Rig
394m

Scrape Burn

Den Knowes

The Scrape
716m

Drumelzier Burn

Den Knowes
Head

River Tweed

Drumelzier Law
668m

Pykestone
Hill 737m

Worm Hill
541m

Hopecarton

Hobcarton Burn

A701

Craig Head
467m

Long Grain Knowe

Long Grain
Knowe 702m

Stanhope

Taberon Law
637m

Laigh Hill
472m

Stanhope
Hope

Stanhope Burn

Lairdside Knowe
499m

Stone Grain

Dollar Law

Birkside Law
595m

Hunt Law
639m

Glentinning Burn

Great Knock
691m

Dun Rig

N

Kilometres 0   1   2
Miles 0   1

PYKESTONE HILL FROM DRUMELZIER

Pykestone Hill (737 m) and its outliers sit above a bend of the River Tweed where, south of Broughton, it starts its more easterly flow towards its final destination at Berwick-on-Tweed. Its near neighbours include the high hills of Dollar Law (Walk 19) and Broad Law (Walk 25).

This longer walk starts from the hamlet of Drumelzier (pronounced "Drumeelyer"), traditional burial place of Merlin, legendary druid, bard and wizard at the court of King Arthur, and who was said to have been stoned to death by the local inhabitants. Search for a venerable thorn bush near Drumelzier Church, said to mark his "grave". There is certainly no lack of forts, towers, settlements and ruined castles in the area, and the property of Merlindale lies just across the Tweed.

To reach the start, turn off the A701 2 km south of Broughton onto the B712 road to Peebles. A further 2.5 km will bring you to Drumelzier. Turn right by the post box (no through road) and drive the short distance to the stone-built hall on the right, where a car may be left.

Walk up to the right of a wooden garage. Where the road divides, take the left-hand track and after passing through a gate, walk up towards the large farm buildings on the right. Approaching the buildings, swing left and make for a gate in a wall across the field. Through the gate, turn sharp left and walk along the edge of a field to reach a gate leading out onto the open moor. Walk up the broad track above the Drumelzier Burn, dropping down eventually to cross the stream by a substantial wooden bridge.

Follow the clear track uphill, and ignoring any side paths, make for the gap

INFORMATION

Distance: 19 km (12 miles).

Map: OS Landranger, sheet 72.

Start and finish: Drumelzier, on B712 at GR135340.

Terrain: On paths and hill track for almost the entire distance. Boots or strong shoes recommended.

Refreshments: None en route. Cafe and hotel in nearby Broughton and further afield in Peebles and Biggar.

Public transport: Bus services along the nearby A701.

The Drumelzier Burn.

between two blocks of larch and pine trees. Above the woods there are two clear tracks, one leading to the right and another heading left, neither of which are shown on the Landranger map. Take the left track and in a few metres turn right and walk up the narrow but clear path heading up the ridge towards Den Knowes. The path passes a number of old disused grouse butts built in the traditional manner with stones and turves.

Higher up on Den Knowes the path meets a Land Rover-type track coming up from the right. Turn left and follow the route as it swings round Den Knowes Head and approaches the flat top and trig point on Pykestone Hill from a northerly direction. This route departs somewhat from that shown on the OS map, but is more easily followed on the ground.

Around two hours walking will have brought you to the summit of Pykestone Hill. During the walk up the ridge, Broad Law, complete with its radio mast and navigation beacon will have been clearly in view, 8.4 km to the south. The seldom seen Polmood Crags which guard its northern shoulder are quite prominent from this angle.

Crest of Tweedie family on church wall above the Tweedie vault.

Cross the fence to the trig point, turn right and follow a track downhill, keeping near to the wire fence. At a col below Pykestone, a short section of old wall could give shelter on a windy day while you eat your lunch. Continue uphill beside the fence following the line of the "Thiefs Road", an old drove road linking Dawyck Mill on the Tweed, with Megget, via Dollar Law.

Towards Long Grain Knowe the "road" swings away from the fence, and wends its way to a saddle before starting its climb towards Dollar Law. Slightly uphill from the saddle, look for and pass through a wooden gate set in a wire fence to the right of the track. The gate is located beyond a prominent shepherd's cairn seen on the far side of the fence.

Walk straight ahead from the gate and in about 100 m meet an obvious track heading down the ridge between the valleys formed by the hill burns of Long Grain and Stone Grain. The track, improving as it goes, swings down the ridge to meet the well-made farm road which leads down to Stanhope some 3.5 km to the north west.

At Stanhope pass through a couple of gates and turn right behind the farmhouse. Walk between farm buildings and follow a grassy track heading north towards the ruined cottage of Hopecarton. Cross a wooden bridge over a burn, pass through a gate, and walk in front of the derelict buildings. Beyond Hopecarton a rough path closely follows the east bank of the River Tweed.

Note an interesting footbridge over the river as you head, now on a grass track, for a cottage hidden behind a shelter belt of trees. Turn left between trees and cottage, and then right in front of the building to a gate which leads out onto an unsurfaced road which heads north east towards Drumelzier. The road soon becomes surfaced and joins the B712. Turn right in

the village and walk up to the hall and to your car, which you left some five hours ago.

The Powsail Burn flowing to meet the Tweed.

This has been a long walk but the chances are you will not have met a soul all day. The mixture of heathery tracks, hill burns, breezy hilltops and distant views of lonely hills is the very essence of Tweedsmuir Hills walking.

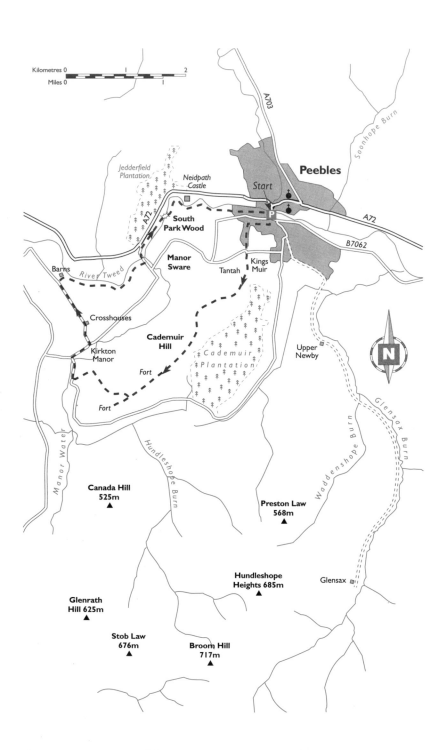

CADEMUIR HILL
AND TWEED WALKWAY

This walk from Peebles explores the ancient hill forts along the Cademuir ridge to the south of the town, and returns along the banks of the River Tweed.

From the large public car park, walk back to the bend just before the bridge and cross the busy road with care. Walk along Caledonian Road and turn left up Edderston Road. Follow the road uphill to its end at the gatehouse of Tantah House. Pass through an iron gate on the right and follow a path beside the wall of Tantah House.

Go through a wooden gate (it can be muddy here) and bear right up a shallow valley to reach the site of an early settlement on Cademuir Hill. Ignore the main path which cuts downhill to the left, and head south-westwards along the ridge to reach two important fortified settlements.

The largest fort, at GR230375, covers an area of some 2.25 hectares and is enclosed within a 3 m thick wall. There are traces of at least 35 timber-framed houses within the fort, which suggests an early Iron Age

INFORMATION

Distance: 16 km (10 miles).

Map: OS Landranger, sheet 73.

Start and finish: Peebles. In the large public car park on the south side of the river by the bridge.

Terrain: Hill tracks, country road and riverside paths. Boots or strong shoes advised.

Refreshments: None en route. Ample selection of cafes, pubs and hotels in Peebles.

Public transport: Regular bus service to Peebles from Edinburgh and other border towns.

Peebles – starting place for many varied walks.

settlement of some significance. The smaller fort occupies the lower western summit of the ridge at GR225371. Outside the ruins of its massive 6 m thick enclosing wall are subsidiary enclosures standing on terraces to the south-west, the south-east, and to the north.

This fort's most interesting feature is the "chevaux de frise" protecting the north-east approach over level ground. This defensive structure still has more than 100 stones standing in the outer side of a small gully.

The stones would have been invisible until attackers had arrived in the gully and were amongst the stones. Result, panic and chaos! The forts, built late BC, were probably abandoned around AD80 after the arrival of the Romans.

Given clear conditions, the views from the Cademuir ridge are impressive. To the south is the Manor Valley, from which a track leads to St Mary's Loch. Somewhat west of south can be seen the higher hills of Tweedsmuir, including Dollar Law at 817 m and Broad Law, with its radio masts and beacon, at 840 m. To the south-east is a large area of high ground known collectively as Hundleshope Heights.

Kirkton Manor Church.

Continue the walk by retracing your steps to the saddle between the two forts. Head north-west down a gully to join a track going left to join a country road. Turn right along the road, cross a bridge over the Manor Water and turn right to Kirkton Manor. Just beyond the church, turn left through white gates, and walk along the access road to the Barns. Pass by the cottages of Crosshouses and walk along the avenue for some 800 m.

Manor Bridge over the Tweed – part of the Tweed Walkway.

Where overhead power lines cross the road, turn right over a stile waymarked "Tweed Walkway". Walk down a path between fields and cross over another stile to the banks of the River Tweed. Turn right and follow the clear and waymarked path downstream to the massive stone Manor Bridge.

Climb the steps at the side of the bridge and cross to the north side of the river. Turn right over a double stile and follow the walkway along the trackbed of the old Caledonian Railway. This line, closed to passenger traffic in 1950, connected Peebles to Carlisle, Edinburgh and Glasgow.

Cross the river again by the old railway viaduct. Turn sharp left into South Park Wood and follow the waymarked path by the riverside all the way back to Peebles. Along the way look for an opportunity to photograph the spectacular 15th century Neidpath Castle standing high above the River Tweed.

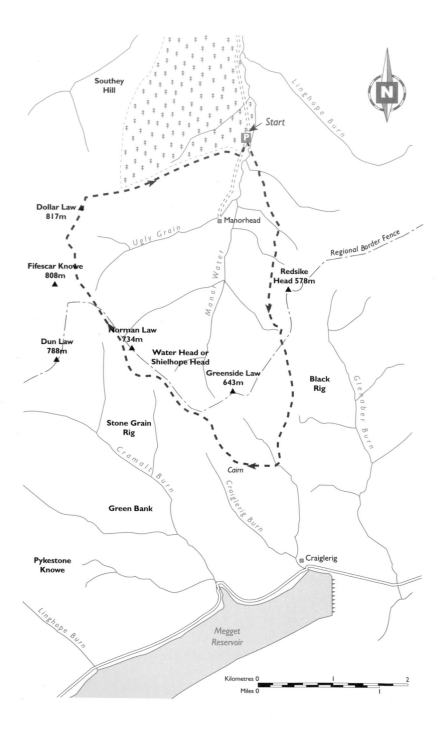

DOLLAR LAW AND THE MANOR VALLEY

If any excuse were needed to climb to the summit of Dollar Law (817 m), then the 14 km drive up the Manor Valley would surely provide such an excuse. That the valley is scenically attractive is without doubt, and since the advent of the motor car the grassy swards beside the Manor Water have been a popular haunt of family picnic parties. Those who come today with camper vans, folding tables and chairs, are but the successors of those who came with travel rugs and picnic hampers in times past.

A glance at the OS map will show that the valley was also a popular place in prehistoric times. There is a string of ancient settlements beyond the east bank of the Manor Water, and a number of forts and settlements, including the so-called MacBeth's Castle, along the west bank. The important 2nd-century farming settlement is to be found in the side valley of the Glenrath Burn.

To reach the start of the walk, turn right at the bottom of Peebles High Street and head west on the A72. In some 3 km, and after passing historic Neidpath Castle, turn left at the junction signposted "Kirkton Manor 4 miles, Manorhead 10 miles". Follow this unclassified road for 14 km up the Manor Valley, firstly by crossing the River Tweed by the Manor Bridge, and then via Kirkton Manor with its attractive church, and past the Black Dwarf's Cottage.

This miniature cottage was allegedly built singlehanded by one David Ritchie, who was so misshapen that he lived the life of a recluse. Sir Walter Scott visited here in 1797 before writing *The Black Dwarf*. Ritchie died in 1811 and is buried in the graveyard at Kirkton Manor.

Towards the head of the valley there is a large plantation on the right of the now much narrower road. Near the southern end of the woodland, at

INFORMATION

Distance: 11 km (7 miles).

Map: OS Landranger, sheets 72 and 73. The complete walk is contained on sheet 5 of the official route map of The Southern Upland Way – eastern section. This is an Ordnance Survey map at 1:50,000.

Start and finish: In a small roadside parking area, or on flat ground down by the Manor Water. At GR199286 near the head of the Manor Valley.

Terrain: On good hill tracks, except for a very short pathless section through heather. Boots or strong shoes advised.

Refreshments: None en route. Ample cafes, pubs and hotels in Peebles.

Public transport: Regular services to Peebles. None down the Manor Valley.

GR199286, there is a small parking area on the left. Park either here, or on the flat ground down by the river.

Start the walk by fording the Manor Water, or crossing it by a nearby footbridge. Head uphill, and keeping to the right of a small wood, pass through a gate and head south along the track leading to St Mary's Loch. As the path gains height there are good views down towards the farm of Manorhead, up to the high ground towards Dollar Law, and into the narrow glen at the head of the Manor Water.

After skirting over the west shoulder of Redsike Head, the path swings down to cross a rather flat area, before arriving at a gate in a wire fence at Foulbrig. This fence forms the boundary between the old counties of Peeblesshire and Selkirkshire. It will be met again later in the walk.

Beyond the gate walk up a well graded track, still following the right of way towards St Mary's Loch. The track soon levels out, and beyond a couple of large piles of stones begins its descent towards the Megget Reservoir.

The farm of Manorhead with the high ground of Dollar Law above.

It is now that a sharp lookout should be kept for a prominent cairn which is 400 m west of the path at GR199246. Leave the track and head directly for the cairn. There is no clear path through the heather, but 10 minutes or so should bring you to this superb vantage point. The stone cairn sits on high ground above old sheepfolds and there is large pile of stones a few metres further west. Given a clear day this is the spot to eat your sandwiches and soak up the views. These include the Cheviot Hills to the south-east and the distant Lakeland Fells far away to the south.

From the pile of stones, head north west to pick up the path which will lead you ultimately to Dollar Law.

The path is faint here but soon improves as it heads first for Shielhope Head, and then up round the western shoulder of Notman Law. The county fence has been generally on your right for some time, and beyond Notman Law you walk beside it for nearly 500 m. The track passes through a gate in the friendly fence and heads for the saddle between Fifescar Knowe and Dollar Law. The route you have been walking since leaving the cairn is a continuation of the Thief's Road, an old drove road coming south from beyond Broughton.

Descending Dollar Law into Manor Valley.

At the saddle, the broad grass track arrives at a gate in a wire fence which runs parallel to an old stone wall. Turn right and walk up beside the wall, to reach the 817 m summit of Dollar Law. What a panoramic view unfolds from this lofty height! To the west, beyond the River Tweed are the rolling tops of the Culter Fells. To the far north may be seen Arthur's Seat and Salisbury Crags above Edinburgh, while to the east lie the prominent Eildon Hills. Broad Law, at 840 m the second highest hill in the Southern Uplands, with the Talla radio beacon near its summit, is just 5 km to the south-west.

Walking up out of the Manor Valley.

To return to the start, continue north for a short distance, then follow the wall in a north-easterly direction, and descend by the edge of the plantation into the Manor Valley. This is a steep descent, so do take extra care.

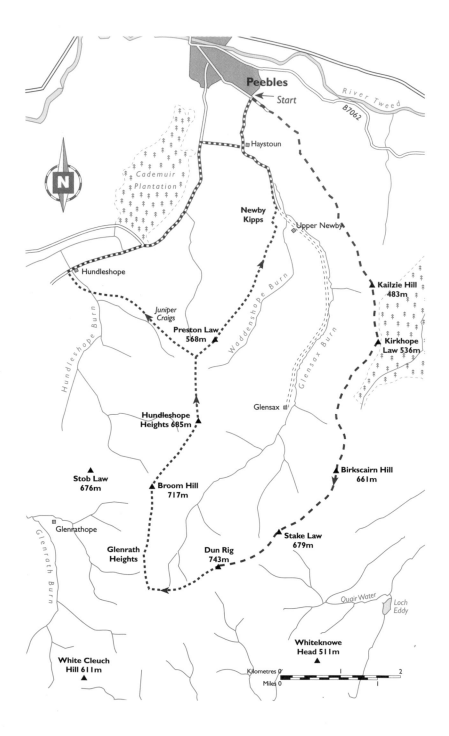

THE GLENSAX ROUND FROM PEEBLES

This longer walk from Peebles has everything the keen hill walker could desire. Firstly, a high-level route along the ridge above the valley of Glensax. This Right of Way between Peebles and Yarrow follows the route of a major Scottish drove road. There are spectacular views from many points along the way. Secondly, and if time and stamina allow, a return route to Peebles made over the high ground of Hundleshope Heights west of Glensax.

To reach the start, travel down Peebles High Street and turn left to cross the bridge over the River Tweed. At the far side of the bridge turn left and almost immediately right into Springhill Road. Continue ahead for 1.2 km and park on either side of the road near to where the tarmac ends. Follow the path forward as indicated by the Scottish Rights of Way Society sign "Public Footpath by Gipsy Glen to Yarrow". After passing an older sign confirming the route to Yarrow the path descends into the Gipsy Glen. Cross the Haystoun Burn by a concrete bridge and climb the steps on the far side of the stream. The clear path now starts its fairly steep ascent, through trees and a couple of gates, out onto the open hillside. During this early part of the walk take an opportunity to catch your breath, and survey the views to the north. The view over the town of Peebles is extensive, with the famous Hydro Hotel prominent. Dunslair

INFORMATION

Distance: 20 km (12.5 miles).

Time: Allow at least 6 hours.

Map: OS Landranger, sheet 73.

Start and finish: Peebles, at the end of Springhill Road.

Terrain: Good hill tracks along the eastern ridge. Less clear along the western ridge if the full circuit option is undertaken. There is a number of gates to open and close and streams to cross. Boots or strong shoes essential.

Refreshments: None en route. Ample selection of cafes, pubs and hotels in Peebles.

Public transport: Regular bus service to Peebles from Edinburgh and other Border towns. Phone (01721) 720151 for details.

The broad Drove Road leading up from the Gipsy Glen.

Heights, complete with radio masts and meteorological station, are clearly seen, as are the Pentland Hills to the south of Edinburgh.

Initially the path, between the walls of the old drove road, keeps to the left of the high ground, and follows the contours round to reach a gate at a col. It is from this point, as it heads up towards Kailzie Hill, that the size and scale of the drove road, can be best appreciated. What you see is but a small section of a long distance route which starts at Falkirk in central Scotland, some 96 km (60 miles) to the north.

The rearing of cattle and sheep was for hundreds of years the mainstay of the Scottish Highland economy. Every autumn the animals were "driven" by long established routes, to cattle markets or trysts. By 1770 the Michaelmas Tryst was established at Falkirk with as many as 30,000 cattle being sold in a week. The chief buyers were English, and it was common for them to hire the sellers to drive the stock to England. It is along such a route south that you are now walking. D. G. Moir, in his book *Scottish Hill Tracks, Old Highways & Drove Roads*, is of the opinion that

this section of "road" follows the line of a much older prehistoric or medieval ridgeway between Peebles and Yarrow.

The track rises steadily towards Kailzie Hill. Near this top the path leaves the confines of the wall and heads for the edge of Cardrona Forest. The track now

The old farm of Glensax.

keeps to the right of a wire fence, firstly over Kirkhope Law, and then a long pull up to the summit of Birkscairn Hill. Both Landranger, sheet 73 and Pathfinder, sheet 460 show the path passing to the west of Birkscairn Hill. The fence however crosses the summit and so does the very clear path. The large pile of stones which marks the summit of Birkscairn Hill would also make a good spot for a lunch stop. The views from here are, to say the least, panoramic. To the west lies the high ground of Hundleshope Heights, to the east, over the valley of the Quair Water, lies the forest of

Elibank and the hills of Minch Moor. To the south are the rolling hills and valleys above St Mary's Loch.

Follow the path beside the fence down from Birkscairn Hill, to the saddle between it and Stake Law. Here a Scottish Rights of Way Society sign confirms the route between Peebles and Yarrow.

Leave the right of way at the saddle, and follow the somewhat dilapidated fence in a south-westerly direction, firstly over Stake Law, and then on to the 743 m summit of Dun Rig. Commanding the high ground to the south of Glensax, Dun Rig was one of a chain of hill and mountain tops on which beacons were lit in celebration of the Queen's Silver Jubilee in 1977.

From the start to the trig point on Dun Rig you will have walked 10 km and had some superb views along the way. It is now that you will have to decide whether to retrace your steps back to Peebles (for most this will be the preferred option) or to continue along the west ridge above Glensax. To complete the walk by the west ridge, first head west to Glenrath Heights, then north over Broom Hill and on to Hundleshope Heights. In just under 1 km due north of the heights a fence is met which leads north-west by the Juniper and Rae Burn to Hundleshope farm, or north-east by Preston Law and Newby Kips down into the Glensax valley. It has to be said though, that in all but the driest of conditions, and in the finest of weathers, this western ridge can be heavy going. There are fine views along the way however, and although it will make for a long and perhaps tiring day, there is the satisfaction of completing "The Round of Glensax".

Glensax in winter.

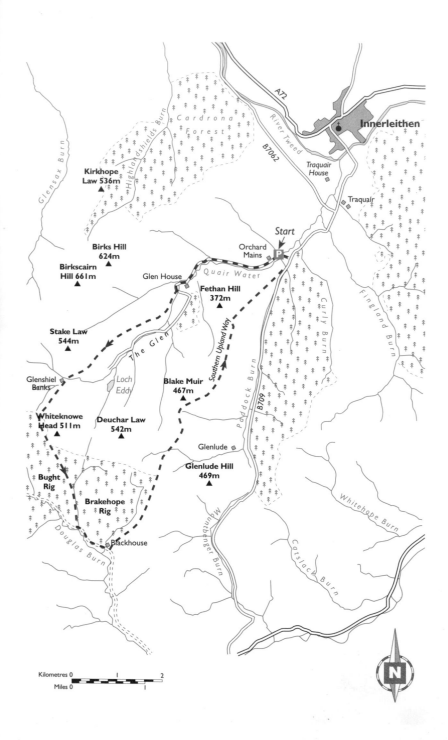

Kilometres 0 — 1 — 2
Miles 0 — 1

N

PEAT HILL AND BLAKE MUIR BY GLENSHIEL BANKS AND THE SOUTHERN UPLAND WAY

This is a longer walk which follows the glen of the Quair Water from Orchard Mains to the isolated cottage of Glenshiel Banks. The route heads up over the shoulder of Peat Hill and down through Craig Douglas forest to the Douglas Burn. From the farm of Blackhouse the Southern Upland Way is followed over Blake Muir to Kirkhouse and Orchard Mains.

To reach the start, turn right off the B709 some 4 km south of Innerleithen at the sign to "Glen House 1¼ miles" and to Orchard Mains. Parking is usually available at Orchard Mains farm, but do ask at the farmhouse for permission. If you cannot park at the farm, you will have to return to the B709.

From the farm walk south-west along the quiet country road, with the Quair Water keeping company on the left as it chatters along towards its meeting with the River Tweed near historic Traquair House. In 2 km

INFORMATION

Distance: 19 km (12 miles).

Map: OS Landranger, sheet 73.

Start and finish: Orchard Mains Farm. Ask at farmhouse for permission.

Terrain: Quiet country road. Clear hill and forest tracks, and the Southern Upland Way. Boots or strong shoes advised.

Refreshments: None en route. Innerleithen, 4 km to the north, has good selection of facilities.

Transport: Regular bus services to Innerleithen.

Note: Dogs must be kept on a lead on this walk.

Gates leading to Glen House.

come to the impressive gateway leading to Glen House. Keep to the right here and walk up the tree-lined road as it makes its way past the rear of turreted Glen House.

This Scottish baronial-style mansion was designed by David Bryce, and during the last war valuable paintings from the National Gallery of Scotland were stored there as a precaution against air-raids on Edinburgh. The house was built in the middle of the 19th century for the Tennant family, who still own the property. The house is currently used as a conference centre, or for shooting parties and paying guests.

Walk through the farm yard with its arched cart sheds, and bear left between a pair of old white metal gates. Turn sharp right beyond the gates and walk up the farm track for 3 km to the isolated cottage at Glenshiel Banks. As you walk steadily uphill through woods and fields, a road can be seen winding along the valley floor leading to the secretive angling water of Loch Eddy.

Walk in front of the cottage at Glenshiel Banks towards a five-bar gate in the far stone wall leading out onto the open moor. Beyond the gate continue south-west, climbing to the ridge ahead.

As height is gained there are fine views down the wooded valley of the Quair Water and to Loch Eddy in its steep-sided glen. Continue climbing to reach a gate at the edge of Craig Douglas Forest. The gate, at GR265304, leads to a path which swings left down a grassy ride between the trees, soon to meet a more definite forest track. In a small clearing direction signs point the way, uphill to Peebles and The Glen, and downhill to Craig Douglas. Follow the Craig Douglas route for 1.5 km to arrive at a wide unsurfaced road which follows the north bank of the Douglas Burn. Turn left and walk along the track to the farm and outbuildings of Blackhouse.

Near to the farm are the remnants of Blackhouse Tower, for centuries a Douglas stronghold. The tower is now fenced off and trees overshadow the ruins. The

Douglas Burn flows nearby on its way to join the Yarrow Water at Craig Douglas. James Hogg, the Scottish poet known as "The Ettrick Shepherd", was herd at Blackhouse from 1790 to 1800. During this time, following a great blizzard, he wrote *Storms*, a vivid account of the men from Blackhouse searching for their sheep. It was through Willie Laidlaw, son of Hogg's employer at Blackhouse, that Hogg was introduced to Sir Walter Scott. They formed a friendship which lasted for the rest of their lives.

Beyond Blackhouse, turn left at a junction to join the Southern Upland Way. Walk through the farmyard, cross the Craighope Burn by a footbridge, and follow the distinct track up through the forest. In 2 km the track breaks out of the woods by stile and gate at the district boundary fence on the ridge south-east of Deuchar Law. The "way" heads generally in a north-easterly direction crossing moorland and hill burns as it makes for the high ground of Blake Muir.

Remains of Blackhouse Tower.

With map and compass in hand, see in the wide panorama, Dunslair Heights above Peebles, Lee Pen, the prominent peak above Innerleithen, and to the north-east the Minch Moor above and beyond Glenlude Forest across the B709. Many other landmarks can be pinpointed along this old drove road. This is grouse shooting country and from August 12th to early December, walkers should be prepared to stand and wait until drives are over.

From Blake Muir follow the marker posts of the SUW down over moorland, across field, and through woods, to come in 3.5 km to the main road near Kirkhouse. Bear left and walk down the road past Traquair Parish Church with its burial aisle of the Stuarts, Earls of Traquair, and many interesting early tombstones. In a further 200 m turn left, cross the bridge over the Quair Water and walk down to the farm of Orchard Mains.

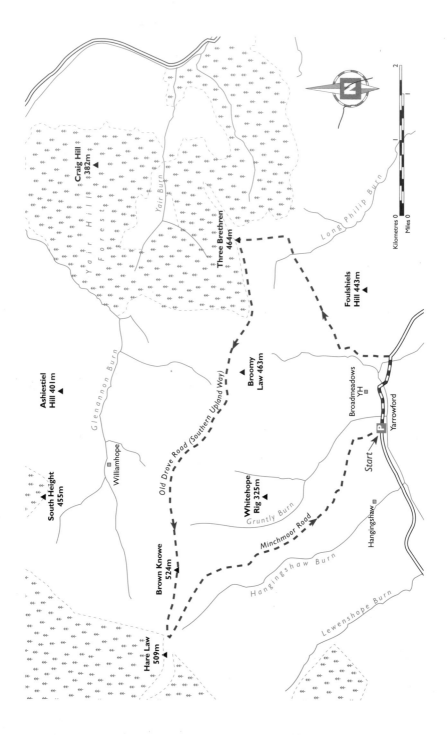

THE THREE BRETHREN AND THE MINCHMOOR

Here is an exhilarating high-level walk in the very heart of Scotland's Border Region. It starts beside Yarrow Water and climbs up to the cairns known as the Three Brethren. It follows the route of the Southern Upland Way and returns down the historic Minchmoor Road. It will be a delight to all those which enjoy the lonely hills and appreciate wide and distant views.

The walk starts from the hamlet of Yarrowford, which lies on the A708 some 6.5 km west of the border town of Selkirk. Park in the small parking area opposite the post box and near to the telephone kiosk. Walk back along the road in the direction of Selkirk with the Yarrow Water flowing busily along on the right. After crossing a second bridge, turn up left by a sign "Public Footpath to Galashiels" and follow the very clear track uphill.

At first the track keeps to the right of a wood through which may be seen Broadmeadows Youth Hostel. Opened in 1931, this was Scotland's first such hostel. After passing through a couple of gates the track turns right (east), leaves the edge of the wood and heads fairly steeply uphill. Near the saddle north of Foulshiels Hill, there are superb views to the south-west up the Yarrow Valley, and to the high hills above St Mary's Loch.

INFORMATION

Distance: 14.5 km (9 miles).

Map: OS Landranger, sheet 73.

Start and finish: Yarrowford on the A708 west of Selkirk.

Terrain: Good paths and hill tracks throughout. Boots or strong shoes advised.

Refreshments: None en route. Ample facilities in Selkirk.

Public transport: Regular services to Selkirk. Minimal service along A708. Phone (01896) 730401 for up to date details.

View up the Yarrow Valley.

On reaching the top of the saddle the cairns of the Three Brethren are seen for the first time at half left. The distinctive Eildon Hills, 13 km to the east, are also clearly in view. Follow the path down into the shallow valley of the Long Philip Burn. Cross the burn and follow the now much narrower path up to a gate in a wire fence. Continue through the heather to meet, in a few hundred metres, a clear track coming up from the right. Turn left along the track and head directly for the cairns.

The Three Brethren.

This direct path to the Three Brethren is a clear one through light heather, and runs parallel to the main path of the Southern Upland Way, which can be seen near the edge of the forest on the right. The stone built cairns stand three metres tall and around two metres in diameter at their base. The hill on which they stand is the meeting of the estates of Yair, of Buccleuch and of the burgh of Selkirk. One cairn stands in each of the three lands.

Each June the cairns are visited by a cavalcade of riders during the Selkirk Common Riding. Please don't be tempted to climb onto the cairns. They have been damaged in the past and stones dislodged. Cross the wire fence by a stile, turn left, and head westwards along the wide track which is the Southern Upland Way.

On the Southern Upland Way.

Stride out, hopefully with a spring in your step, along the broad "road" by the edge of the forest. Take care not to follow a right hand turn into the forest, but keep to the main track, following the Southern Upland Way marker posts. As the track leaves the forest edge it follows a well maintained wall round the north shoulder of Broomy Law. The views to the north from along this section of the walk can only be described as stunning.

Follow the grassy path, with the wall still on your left, down past a plantation of twisted and windblown old pine trees, into a little glen. Cross over a stile and following the directions of a marker post, bear right and head uphill towards the summit of Brown Knowe.

This section of the route also forms part of one of the many old drove roads which pass through the borders. Cattle sold to English buyers at Scottish markets or "trysts", were driven "on the hoof", over long distances into England.

The summit of Brown Knowe (524 m) marks the highest point on the walk. There are gates here and a pile of stones to form a cairn. The views in all directions are wide, distant, and memorable. The way now descends towards the forest of Elibank and Traquair. As the route reaches the corner of the forest, turn hard left by a Southern Upland Way marker post, and head down the Minchmoor Road.

The "road" goes for some 4 km down the ridge between Hangingshaw Burn and Gruntly Burn. At first the track keeps to the right (west) of the ridge and through heather. Halfway down and at a col, the path switches to the left side of the ridge, and continues towards the valley on an easy grass track. Lower still the path continues to the left of the trees of Hangingshaw Wood.

Follow the path as it goes right, through a gate, and enters the wood. Soon the path turns down left and comes out into the open, above some houses. Turn right and then left, to pass between the houses and the red painted village hall to reach the main road and your waiting car.

When you have completed this walk you will have tasted the very essence of Border hill walking, and following in the footsteps of kings and fighting men. Edward the First travelled this way in 1296, and after the battle of Philiphaugh in 1645, the defeated Marquis of Montrose and the remnants of his Cavalier army fled up the road down which you have just walked.

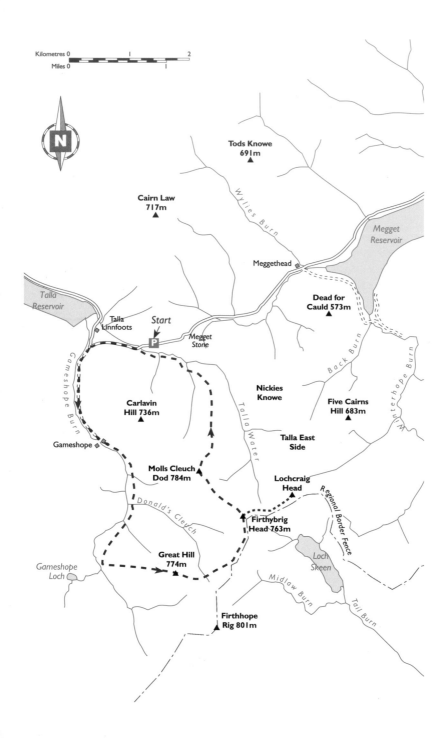

Kilometres 0   1   2
Miles 0   1

N

Tods Knowe
691m
▲

Cairn Law
717m
▲

Wylies Burn

*Megget
Reservoir*

Meggethead

*Talla
Reservoir*

Dead for
Cauld 573m
▲

Talla
Linnfoots

Start
P

Megget
Stone

Back Burn

Winterhope Burn

Gameshope Burn

Nickies
Knowe

Five Cairns
Hill 683m
▲

Carlavin
Hill 736m
▲

Talla Water

Gameshope

Talla East
Side

Molls Cleuch
Dod 784m
▲

Lochcraig
Head
▲

Donald's Cleuch

Firthybrig
Head 763m
▲

Regional Border Fence

*Gameshope
Loch*

Great Hill
774m
▲

*Loch
Skeen*

Midlaw Burn

Tail Burn

Firthhope
Rig 801m
▲

GAMES HOPE GLEN AND THE FIRTHYBRIG RIDGE

INFORMATION

Distance: 13 km (8 miles).

Map: OS Landranger, sheets 72, 78 and 79. The complete walk can be followed on the official map of The Southern Upland Way, eastern section, sheet 4.

Start and finish: A rough lay-by on the north side of the road above Talla Linnfoot at GR NT142201.

Terrain: Rough farm track, pathless near the head of Games Hope Glen, a steep hill climb, and a very fine ridge walk. Boots or strong shoes essential.

Refreshments: None en route. Nearest at St Mary's Loch.

Public transport: None nearby.

The unclassified and mainly single track road linking Tweedsmuir on the A701 and the A708 at St Mary's Loch, gives access to a number of walking possibilities in the Tweedsmuir Hills. The road, which makes its way along the northern shore of both the Talla and Megget reservoirs, does not see many cars in a day, particularly outside the holiday season. By sensible parking, walks can be enjoyed far from the coaches, mini-buses and cars that fill the car parks at the Grey Mare's Tail.

This walk starts up the Games Hope Glen from Talla Linnfoot. It climbs the steep eastern shoulder of Great Hill and makes for Donald's Cleuch Head. A fine broad ridge is followed to Molls Cleuch Dod, from where a descent is made to the road. (Cleuch: a narrow gully with a burn.)

Reach the start by making for a small car parking area at GR NT142201 (Landranger 72). If driving east from Tweedsmuir, climb the steep single track road up from Talla Linnfoot, cross the Talla Water by a stone bridge, and parking is available in the lay-by on the left. If driving west from St Mary's Loch, the parking spot is on the right, 1 km beyond the Megget Stone.

Having parked your car with care, walk down the winding single track road towards Talla Linnfoot. On the way downhill there are fine views of Talla Reservoir with its surrounding hills and forests. At the

Talla Reservoir.

bottom of the hill, and at a right hand bend, turn left through an iron gate and walk up the broad rough farm track into Games Hope Glen.

Gameshope Burn.

With the rushing waters of the Games Hope Burn on the right, and the boulder-strewn steep side of Carlavin Hill on the left, the narrow valley could easily be mistaken for a remote highland glen. In 2 km the twisting track arrives opposite the derelict cottage of Gameshope with its equally derelict footbridge across the burn. It must have been a lonely life for those who lived here in the past.

This marks the end of the main farm track. Beyond a large new feed store, a faint path continues beside the Games Hope Burn, crossing a number of small feeder burns as it heads towards a large rectangular sheepfold or intake field. Nearby are the remains of an old footbridge over the burn. At this point bear slightly left, away from the stream, where a rough path will be found leading uphill to a gate in a wire fence.

Once through the gate, cross Donald's Cleuch Burn by a wooden footbridge. Beyond the footbridge there appears to be no clear path. Head away from the Games Hope Burn again, and make your way diagonally across a rather damp plateau, past occasional peat hags, and by way of a small round sheepfold, to arrive at a gateway in a broken fence. There are old wooden sheep pens nearby and a metal feed store further south. It's around 1.5 km from the Donald's Cleuch footbridge to the fence, so don't give up hope!

Turn up left and follow the broken fence eastwards to the rounded top of Great Hill. This steep climb of some 240 m will take about 45 minutes. Don't rush, but take your time and stop to admire the surrounding scenery – frequently! Look back, for instance, over the nearby Gameshope Loch and pick out the "golf ball" radar domes on Lowther Hill, and the aerial array atop Green Lowther, 30 km away to the south west.

Once on the breezy summit of Great Hill there are good views in all directions. Note particularly the bulky outline of Hart Fell to the south-west, and the prominent 800 m summit of Lochcraig Head above Loch Skeen 2.5 km away to the north-east. Follow the old broken fence over the top of Great Hill, and at a depression beyond, leave the fence and bear left to follow an obvious path above Donald's Cleuch to reach a dilapidated wall and fence on the ridge of Donald's Cleuch Head.

Turn left (north) and follow a track beside the wall to the 763 m top of Firthybrig Head. This is fine ridge walking, with the lonely hills rolling away in all directions as far as the eye can see, and as is so often the case in the Border hills, the triple peaks of the Eildon Hills can be clearly seen, 40 km away to the north-east.

On Firthybrig Head the regional boundary wall and fence recently followed heads, at a T-junction, east to Lochcraig Head. A diversion may be made to Lochcraig Head, from where there are fine views of the wild scenery around Loch Skeen. Your route however continues north-west for a further scenic kilometre to the summit of Molls Cleuch Dod.

Firthybrig Head from the north.

At the summit a fairly large cairn has been built of stones from the broken wall. Turn right, through a gap in the wall and walk towards another, smaller cairn, across the hill top. Walk over the brow of the hill, and heading north, meet a new fence. Turn right and follow the fence to a gate at its eastern end.

Go through the gate and follow a tractor track down the ridge between Molls Cleuch and Talla Water. Initially the track keeps close to the fence, but as the fence swings away right, the track makes for a crossing of Molls Cleuch Burn.

Once across the burn a rough farm track leads to a large feed or hay shed. Beyond the shed an improving track leads to the road by the stone bridge over the Talla Water, and the end of what will have been a memorable day out in the Tweedsmuir Hills.

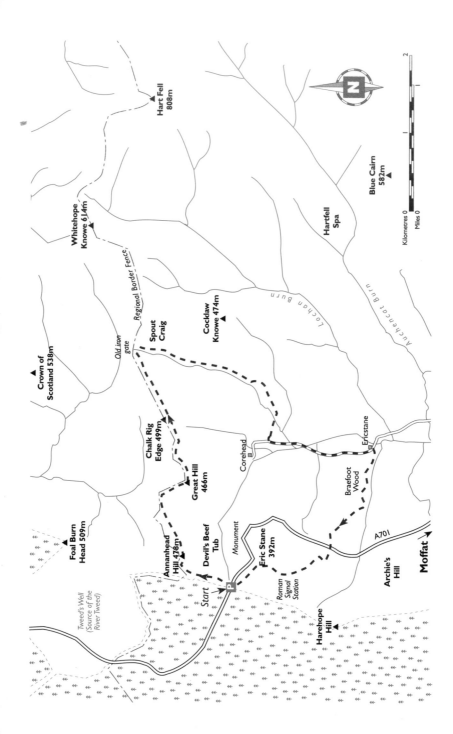

Hart Fell
808m

Blue Cairn
582m

Hartfell
Spa

Whitehope
Knowe 614m

Regional Border Fence

Old iron gate

Spout
Craig

Cocklaw
Knowe 474m

Lochan Burn

Auchencat Burn

Crown of
Scotland 538m

Chalk Rig
Edge 499m

Great Hill
466m

Corehead

Ericstane

Braefoot
Wood

Foal Burn
Head 509m

Annanhead
Hill 478m

Devil's Beef
Tub

Monument

Eric Stane
392m

A701

Moffat

Archie's
Hill

Start

P

Tweed's Well
(Source of the
River Tweed)

Roman
Signal
Station

Harehope
Hill

Kilometres 0

Miles 0

THE DEVIL'S BEEF TUB

Eight kilometres north of the busy border town of Moffat lies the Devil's Beef Tub, a 250 m deep, steep-sided hollow among wild and barren hills, yet close to the A701. This walk takes advantage of a lay-by on the main road at an altitude of 392 m to gain the summit of Annanhead Hill at 479 m.

Beyond Annanhead Hill the route follows the boundary wall and fence between Borders Region and Dumfries and Galloway Region to the col at the north-east end of Chalk Rig Edge. A faint path is followed down the valley of Tweed Hope and then by surfaced track to Ericstane. The main road is regained by a track heading uphill directly from the farm.

To reach the start, drive up the A701 from the spa town of Moffat for some 8 km. Where the road straightens out beyond the Beef Tub view point, there is a lay-by on the right-hand side of the road of the road where a car may be parked. A little further ahead there is a wide access gateway leading into Raccleuch Forest.

To the right of the main forest gate is an older slide gate. Go through the slide gate and in 20 m or so

INFORMATION

Distance: 11.5 km (7 miles).

Map: OS Landranger, sheet 78, and Pathfinder, sheet 483.

Start and finish: At lay-by on A701 north of the Beef Tub view point.

Terrain: Hill paths (some faint), country lanes and main road. Boots or strong shoes recommended.

Refreshments: None en route. Ample cafes, pubs and hotels in nearby Moffat.

Public transport: Bus services to and from Moffat.

The Devil's Beef Tub.

climb over a short section of wooden fence. Walk uphill, keeping to the right of the forest fence, to reach the trig point on the grassy top of Annanhead Hill. From here walk north-east over Peat Knowes, now with the wall and fence of the regional boundary on your left. Path and wall come together at the head of a rough gully. Walk carefully down to the edge of the gully for fine views into the Beef Tub below.

Tradition has it that the Beef Tub, known in earlier time as the "Corrie of Annan", was used in the 16th century by the Johnstones to hoard stolen cattle. In spite of its depth and steep sides, the hardy black-faced sheep graze its flanks. The "Moffat Ram" overlooking Moffat High Street symbolises the town's role as a sheep and wool trading centre, still remembered at the annual installation of the Shepherd and his Lass for the local Gala Week.

Return to the head of the gully and follow the wall and fence east, up and over Great Hill, and out and along the ridge of Chalk Rig Edge. The views from along the ridge are wide and distant. To the north stretches hill and moorland towards Tweedsmuir and the Fruid Reservoir. The 538 m high hill named Crown of Scotland can be picked out, a grand sounding name for a not particularly inspiring looking hill.

The view to the east is dominated by the gully-indented, whale-backed outline of Hart Fell. In one of its gullies, that of the Auchencat Burn, can be found Hartfell Spa. The mineral qualities of the water were discovered by one John Williamson in 1748 and there were many who made the journey to "cure" their ailments. Looking south from Chalk Rig Edge there are fine views down upper Annandale towards Moffat.

At the north-east end of the ridge the path goes downhill to a col below the rocky outcrops of Spout Craig. Where the fence makes a right-hand bend, find a rusty iron gate set in new fencing. Turn right here, and walk away from the gate, soon to pick up a track heading south, and to the left of a developing burn.

This is very much a "come and go" path. It is clearly
marked on the 1:25,000 Pathfinder, sheet 483, but
now keeps losing itself in grass and bracken. There are
a number of old stone sheep shelters and sheepfolds as
you head downhill, keeping always to the ground on
the left of the Tweedhope Burn with its attractive
little waterfalls.

At the bottom of the valley pass through
a gate to the left of a small wood. Bear
right and follow the edge of the wood to
a second gate. From the gate, walk down
hill between wire fences to a large round
sheepfold. At the wall beyond the
sheepfold, turn right, towards the burn,
and then left over a gate or fence beside
the stream.

In the field beyond, bear right, ford the
stream and pass through a metal gate.
Walk over a couple of small fields to gain
the surfaced road to the right of a large
hay shed south of the farm of Corehead.
Turn left and follow the farm road for a
pleasant 1.5 km walk to the farm of
Ericstane.

Just before the farm buildings, turn right
through a gate and head uphill on a
broad farm track to the right of
woodland. Past the empty farm buildings of Braefoot
the track turns right beyond a gate and follows a stone
wall almost all the way up to a metal gate at the A701.

Top: Plaque on Postie Stone
near Moffat.

Bottom: Postie Stone near
Moffat.

From this point there is a choice of route to the lay-by
from which you started. Either walk up the main road
past the Beef Tub view point with its direction
indicator and Covenanter memorial stone, or cross the
road with care and follow a track over Ericstane Hill
past the site of a Roman signal station. This signal
station was connected with troop movements along
the Roman road between Carlisle and the Clyde. A
gate on the north side of the hill gives out onto the
road almost opposite the lay-by, and your waiting car.

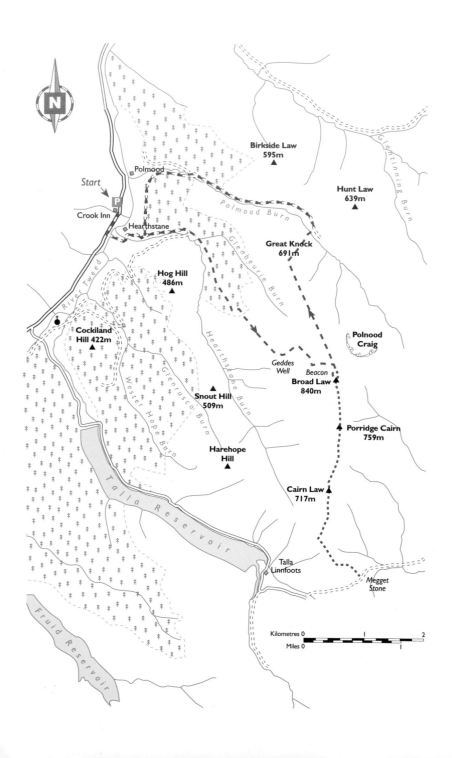

N

Birkside Law
595m
▲

Hunt Law
639m
▲

Polmood

Start

P

Crook Inn

Hearthstane

Polmood Burn

Great Knock
691m
▲

Glenheurie Burn

Hog Hill
486m
▲

River Tweed

Cockiland
Hill 422m
▲

Wester Hope Burn

Glenrusco Burn

Hearthstane Burn

Polnood
Craig

Geddes
Well

Beacon
Broad Law
840m

Snout Hill
509m
▲

Porridge Cairn
759m
▲

Harehope
Hill
▲

Talla Reservoir

Cairn Law
717m
▲

Talla
Linnfoots

Megget
Stone

Fruid Reservoir

Kilometres 0   1   2
Miles 0   1

BROAD LAW

I n 1891 the Scottish Mountaineering Club held its first official meet at the Crook Inn in order to climb Broad Law. The summit, at 840 m, is the second highest in southern Scotland, being only 3 m below the height of Merrick, some 96 km away to the south-west in Galloway.

The Crook Inn, which lies on the A701 2.4 km north of Tweedsmuir, is Scotland's oldest licensed inn dating from 1604. It is a former coaching inn and in the 17th century was a clandestine meeting place for Covenanters. Robert Burns, a regular visitor, wrote his poem *Willie Wastles Wife* in the kitchen (now the bar) of the Crook, and the history and rugged scenery of the area inspired some of the works of Sir Walter Scott.

John Buchan (1875–1940), the Scottish politician and author, has local family connections. He set many of his adventure novels in the district and took the title Lord Tweedsmuir when he was made a peer. There is an interesting John Buchan museum in nearby Broughton which is open 1400–1700, 1 May to mid October.

Park to the rear of the Crook Inn car park. Walk out to the road, turn right and in 300 m turn left and cross a bridge over the infant River Tweed, signposted Hearthstane. Walk up the farm road, turn left over a

INFORMATION

Distance: 13 km (8 miles).

Map: OS Landranger, sheet 72.

Start and finish: At the Crook Inn on the A701, 22 km north of Moffat.

Terrain: On road and good hill tracks except along the ridge between Broad Law and Great Knock, and down to the Polmood Burn. Boots or strong shoes recommended.

Refreshments: None en route. Bar meals, etc. at the Crook Inn. Ample selection of pubs, cafes and hotels in Moffat, Peebles or Biggar.

Public transport: Minimal.

Crook Inn.

bridge then right to follow the main track up to the corner of a wood. Continue on the track along the edge of the wood first heading east, then south-east, keeping the Hearthstane Burn on your right.

Culter Fell from Broad Law.

After crossing a small footbridge the track rises through the wood to break out onto the open hillside at the 500 m contour. The track climbs more steeply now, rising 250 m in just 1 km. There are numbered marker posts on each side of the track all the way to the summit, this being the access road to the Civil Aviation Authorities' Talla radio beacon which is just north of the Broad Law cairn.

This navigation beacon is used by shuttle and other flights in and out of the Scottish area. There are other civil radio transmitters nearby. It you wish to take a compass bearing here, move well away as the large metal structure of the beacon can have a dramatic effect on your compass! The views from the summit cairn are, on a clear day, panoramic. To the south-east are the Cheviot Hills, to the south the Lakeland Fells, and to the west the Culter Fells south of Biggar.

From Broad Law head just west of north down the broad ridge as far as Great Knock. There is a faint and intermittent path down the ridge, but in any case it is an easy walk in light heather. From Great Knock make your way down into the valley of the Polmood Burn. It is a steep and pathless descent so take extra care with your footing.

Cross the Polmood Burn at any convenient spot and turn left along a clear track coming down from the valley head. Follow the track in its steep-sided glen all the way down to a large sheepfold on the right. Bear left here, cross the Polmood Burn by a ford and follow a path round the edge of a wood to arrive at Hearthstane farm. Beyond the farm turn right for the main road and back to your car at the Crook Inn – and afternoon tea perhaps.

An alternative ascent of Broad Law can be made very easily from the Megget Stone, which marks the high point on the unclassified road between Tweedsmuir and St Mary's Loch. This start point is at 452 m so there is only 388 m left to go to the top. The route follows the Peebles–Selkirk boundary fence all the way to the summit of Broad Law, a distance of some 4 km.

INDEX

Opposite: Talla Reservoir.

Other titles in this series

25 Walks – In and Around Aberdeen
25 Walks – Deeside
25 Walks – Dumfries and Galloway
25 Walks – Edinburgh and Lothian
25 Walks – Fife
25 Walks – In and Around Glasgow
25 Walks – Highland Perthshire
25 Walks – The Trossachs

Other titles in preparation

25 Walks – The Chilterns
25 Walks – The Cotswolds
25 Walks – The Western Isles
25 Walks – The Yorkshire Dales

Long distance guides published by HMSO

The West Highland Way – Official Guide
The Southern Upland Way – Official Guide

HMSO Bookshops
71 Lothian Road, Edinburgh EH3 9AZ
0131-228 4181 Fax 0131-229 2734
49 High Holborn, London WC1V 6HB
(counter service only)
0171-873 0011 Fax 0171-831 1326
68–69 Bull Street, Birmingham B4 6AD
0121-236 9696 Fax 0121-236 9699
33 Wine Street, Bristol BS1 2BQ
0117 9264306 Fax 0117 9294515
9-21 Princess Street, Manchester M60 8AS
0161-834 7201 Fax 0161-833 0634
16 Arthur Street, Belfast BT1 4GD
01232 238451 Fax 01232 235401
The HMSO Oriel Bookshop, The Friary,
Cardiff CF1 4AA
01222 395548 Fax 01222 384347

HMSO publications are available from:

HMSO Publications Centre
(Mail, fax and telephone orders only)
PO Box 276, London SW8 5DT
Telephone orders 0171-873 9090
General enquiries 0171-873 0011
(queuing system in operation for both numbers)
Fax orders 0171-873 8200

HMSO's Accredited Agents
(see Yellow Pages)

and through good booksellers